KV-108-008

Secret Practices

*Interdisciplinary Work in
Child Welfare*

DR ALEXIS A. TAYLOR

UPFRONT PUBLISHING
LEICESTERSHIRE

Secret Practices
Copyright © Dr Alexis A. Taylor 2003

All rights reserved

ISBN 1-84426-158-1

First published 2003 by
UPFRONT PUBLISHING LTD
Leicestershire

Typeset in Bembo by
Bookcraft Ltd, Stroud, Gloucestershire
Printed by Lightning Source

To Finlay and Hollie
In memory of Trevor Taylor, 1942–1993

SECRET PRACTICES
Interdisciplinary Work in Child Welfare

ACKNOWLEDGMENTS

I owe an immeasurable debt of gratitude to the academic supervisors who struggled with me on my research journey: Dr Martyn Jones, and Dr Jean Packman of the University of Exeter, Devon, UK. Also to people who advised me on my earlier writing: Dr R Bullock, Ms S Glennie, Dr R Gomm, Ms A Hutton, Dr P Kay, Ms S Cardamitis, and Dr W Stainton Rogers.

My thanks to friends and colleagues for their support including: Penny Craig, Gill Downham, Ernistine Heron, Rosemary Huxtable, John Ingham, Maureen Kennard, Joy Fisher, Dave Rollason, Deb Parker, Elaine Parry, Julie Philips, and Dr Peter Pope.

The governors and officers in the residential unit were enthusiastic and generous with their time. The Community Health Service Trust gave permission to quote from their records.

ABOUT THE AUTHOR

After 5 years working in the health sector Alexis Taylor qualified in Social Work in 1973. She has worked with children and families in locality, hospital and child mental health settings specialising in abuse and neglect. She was a Chair of interdisciplinary child protection meetings for 9 years with a special interest in emotional and psychological harm. Following a period as an independent consultant modernising childcare services and assessing professional performance in Britain and Africa she gained a qualification in tropical community medicine. Her focus is currently on the health, welfare, and rights of children living in low resource countries.

This book is an ethnography produced solely from the written products of a social world. (The empirical research studied the case records of a child mental health team.)

Key objectives

To show a multidisciplinary social world at work and demonstrate the vital importance of the language used to describe consumers of social and health care. To demonstrate how written documents compiled by professionals can be used to evaluate performance. To present new theory (about interdisciplinary decision making) derived from empirical material. To illustrate how major themes emerge from detailed research. (In this instance how children's rights are being infringed.)

ABOUT THE BOOK

Key themes

Child welfare services need radical alteration. A new 'architecture of care' must be built on the ashes of the current monolithic institutions and professional tribes.

The evidence presented challenges the quality of some of the assessments made by multidisciplinary groups of workers. There are salutary messages for child welfare practitioners and policy makers. Professional work can be self-serving rather than 'in the best interests of the child'. Power struggles between professionals can distort their accounts of what is going on for a child. The components of professional decisions are explored in a novel way, and changes to practice are suggested.

Reasons why this is a valuable publication

In addition to demonstrating some of the challenges and delights of ethnographic work, it considers the effectiveness of 'joined up thinking', and collaboration between child welfare disciplines. It argues that children are powerless in mental health systems. (This used to apply to adult service users.) It should, at the very least, lead child mental health teams to enquire: 'Is this true for us'?

FOREWORD

In this book, Alexis Taylor shows how scrutiny of documents taken from the files of a child mental health agency can offer insights into the ways in which professionals conduct their work, make decisions and interact with each other. Her study examined the records over a period of ten years, of the assessment and treatment of adolescent girls referred for a range of problems at home and/or school. The aim of the study was to build up a picture of the social practices involved, looking particularly at the operation of power and how this enabled the management of conflict, in order to sustain the agency in question.

This book examines in fine detail how control was imposed, resisted and negotiated within and between professional disciplines, and in the dealings these practitioners had with the adolescent girls that were referred to them and their families. Ostensibly, the agency provided a service to help 'troubled and troublesome' adolescent girls overcome the difficulties they were facing, and offered treatment for their mental health problems. What emerges from Taylor's analysis, however, is quite another picture of what was going on. This includes a great deal of power mongering and dispute over control, and jockeying for dominance within interprofessional hierarchies, extensive examples of defensive and self-serving practice, the medicalisation of the girls' problems in order to avoid the stigmatisation for their families of social work intervention, or for the girls of being labelled 'delinquent'. Crucially, Taylor offers evidence that treating the girls' behaviour and other symptoms as 'the problem' was being used to deflect attention away from alternative explanations – notably, in many cases, the sexual abuse to which they were being subjected.

This book offers a number of salutary messages for both practitioners and policy makers. Alexis Taylor's painstaking work raises disturbing questions about the way 'the best interests of the child' arguments are often used to warrant practices and decisions which serve not children's but adult's interests, and which can all too often further subject children to the abuse of adult power. Specifically, Taylor argues that 'children in distress are being differentiated by the artful use of language'. She concludes that this differentiation seldom serves its subjects at all well and that we need to look for a radically new way of helping and supporting the young, which better meets their needs and more properly respects their rights. This, she acknowledges, will require considerable courage, since it will entail dismantling some of our current institutions and replacing them with a new and more productive, more humane and more effective 'architecture of care'.

I very much hope that her work can contribute to this goal. I strongly agree with Taylor's assessment that 'the state is not providing well for its most challenging children' and that it is about time we called a halt to its abusive practices and put something a lot better in their place. Whether we will find the courage to do so, I am not so sure. This is not an easy book to read: it is deliberately discomforting. Let us hope, then, that we can use the unease it generates to take action, rather than simply being so embarrassed that we quickly draw a veil over her findings, just as the records she scrutinised all too often acted to obscure what people found too disturbing to tackle.

A good start would be – as she has so very potently demonstrated – for all of us to become much more careful about the language we use when writing about the young, whether as academics, as teachers, as policy makers or as practitioners. We are becoming increasingly aware that language is never 'natural' or 'innocent' but a powerful means of constructing realities. Like Mary Shelley in her parable of Frankenstein's monster, Taylor reminds us that we need to take care about the horrors that can be perpetrated on, as well as by, the 'monsters' we so construct.

Wendy Stainton Rogers,
School of Health and Social Welfare,
The Open University

PREFACE

This book shares some of the exploration and the conclusions of a research journey which began in 1989. I was curious about the work of a residential unit which offered shared care to families with children described as emotionally disturbed. It appeared to be a pre-existing model of service provision that matched some of the intentions of the 1989 Children Act.

The end product of the research process stands in fascinating contrast to those original interests. It melds together a portrait of a social world (an ethnography) and emergent theory about the construction of professional decisions. It shares ways for individual practitioners, their managers, and interagency teams to think about their practices before implementing plans that will have significant impact on service users.

The analysis produced compelling questions about child mental health services, and should inspire and empower those who advocate for the rights of children. Practitioners in child mental health services will be moved to ask: 'Is this true for us?'

Most important of all, the evidence produced compelling reasons for dismantling the current child welfare system in the UK and introducing a simple, child friendly architecture of support and care.

Readership

The book will be relevant to practitioners, managers, commissioners, and designers in human welfare organisations. Those developing interagency working methods or evaluating the performance of multidisciplinary teams may be attracted to the analysis of processes of interaction and the grounded theory of decision making. It is pertinent to students of Public Policy, Ethics of Social Welfare and Management. The archaeology and critical evaluation of a child mental health agency is pertinent to the several disciplines currently engaged in providing services dedicated to children's emotional and psychological well-being – child psychiatrists, community psychiatric nurses, psychologists and social workers. Other readers may include those researching social life, ethnographers and analysts of discourse and text.

Contents

INTRODUCTION

Severe psychotic illness ... sudden refusal to attend school ... at home exposed to intense and not very helpful relationships of a kind which are known to produce relapse, not parents fault, just one of those unfortunate things ... the most practical solution is the (residential unit) where Elaine (13.2)* would get psychiatric supervision ... good support ... specialised management and understanding ... be maintained in full-time education ... in this way I think we could give this unfortunate but very bright girl an opportunity to attain. (Letter from a child and adolescent psychiatrist)

This book demonstrates how auditors who are not experts in a particular field can use case records to access the places in human service organisations where significant decisions are taken by one or more professional workers. A detailed description of how people in a multidisciplinary team conduct their business contributes to ways of thinking about professional work. Suggestions are made for improving the quality of interdisciplinary practice by using two empirically grounded models of decision making (Taylor, 1999). These can be applied when the next intervention would have a major impact on consumers (Taylor, 2000).

The research domain was a Child and Adolescent Mental Health Team (CAMHT). Formerly known as a child guidance clinic it remained largely unchanged in personnel, clientele and ideology for the decade studied (1977 to 1988). This was a social world that resisted intrusion. Observation of people at work or the interview of clients was forbidden. Instead, permission was given for the release of documents and case records concerning all the children who were placed in a particular residential unit during the decade. Quotations from the records are used throughout the book and the primary documentary sources are introduced in Chapter I.

---

* Figures indicate age in years and months.

This apparently quintessentially child-centred world presented many paradoxes: lack of synergy between them and resistance to contact with outside influences outweighed the kindness, hard work and wealth of experience of the workers. They were also very poor at listening to children (Chapter VII), which, when coupled with the essentially disciplinary function of the agency (Chapter VI), suggested that contemporary critiques of adult mental health services must be extended to child mental health domains. Children particularly needed advocates when their carers declined to become involved in the task of altering unsatisfactory or dangerous situations.

Secrecy is a theme that emerges in almost every chapter. The total confidentiality surrounding the agency was unhelpful, not least because it prevented professional performance appraisal. Whilst agencies must respect a child's need for privacy, it is clear that they do not benefit from total secrecy. There are many indicators that most of the ninety-nine young people studied may have been victims of sexual abuse. This opened up the possibility that the sense that the multidisciplinary team was making of children's situations was nonsense. In turn, powerful evidence emerged that inadequate performance in the initial work with children was not recognised. Engaging the child mental health services in a debate on these issues will be the next critical step for those creating strategic plans for children.

There are some key messages about how health and welfare services could be provided to an extremely vulnerable group of children and young people, and support for a much more radical approach. The review of child mental health services, *Together we Stand* (NHS/HAS, 1995), presented an expanded four-tiered design for the service. The third and forth tiers will preserve the old world which frames children's distress in unhelpful psychobabble and dramatically disenfranchises them. It is highly likely that the primary and secondary services will define many more children as mentally ill in order to justify service provision.

Chapter VI shows that there is little difference between the clientele of a local Child and Adolescent Mental Health Service (CAMHS) and a Social Services Department (SSD). Therefore, there is no benefit in continued separation. The time has come to embed the valuable elements of the CAMHS within a new range of services for children and their carers, and consign the rest of the seventy-year-old industry to history.

The first chapter shows how to rummage in a disciplined manner in case notes and standard documents. As an experimental research method, it had several disadvantages. It was laborious, because the sample was too large, and it was difficult to manage the multitude of ideas that emerged. It was also hard to leave tracts of fascinating text behind as the generalities emerged. Theory and hypotheses were not applied to the data but were developed from it. So, the fields into which the researcher might delve were unconstrained by the restrictions normally derived from a literature review. Consequently, for long periods there was little clear direction to the work. It became important to set an end point, limit the number of themes, and review the literature of some of the dominant fields. However, because an interest in decision-making processes emerged close to the end point, that extensive literature remains largely neglected. Despite all these disadvantages, some well-grounded findings have provided:

- A simple method that can be used with confidence by naïve enquirers into professional performance.
- An applied practice to improve multi-agency decision taking in a case.
- Evidence that children in mental health settings are seriously disempowered.

The buzz gained from being introduced to new concepts and 'grounded theory' (Glaser and Strauss, 1967) is enduring. The shift from an initial proposition to describe and evaluate the outcomes of an apparently unusual residential institution for adolescents, to formulating theories about professional performance was exciting and continually engaging. The exposure of this writing to the community of thinkers about child welfare work, in particular, is a necessary step towards testing some of the following ideas:

- Case records can assist in performance evaluation and service development.
- Work undertaken by professional personnel is the least likely

to be evaluated. Some clients could avoid unnecessary interventions if the quality of the work to date is rigorously reviewed before implementing different and perhaps more costly recipes for change.

- Attention should be paid to the information that is discarded in assessments because this may be done in order to match the client to the agency's resources.
- Even in client-centred organisations, the voice of the client can be weak.
- Children use three types of 'hints' in an attempt to influence decisions.
- Strict confidentiality in child welfare is unhelpful.

Practice methods for application at points where a change in service delivery would have a significant impact on the outcomes for clients are presented. (In these cases, children were removed from the full-time care of their parents.) The model can be applied by practitioners and their managers to single cases and to interagency group work. The patterning of interdisciplinary collaboration observed in the CAMHT showed that groups could monitor corporate performance (Chapter X). Additionally, a novel design emerged which would bring the needs of wider communities to attention, even when the interface is between the agency and an individual service user.

The analysis was set against the broad canvas of new UK legislation for children in the 1989 Children Act. The welfare of the child is paramount, and every effort is made to establish a cooperative partnership with carers. The CAMHT illustrates why professional practice had to be challenged and some of the consequences when welfare agencies are untouched by this philosophy.

The ethnography created a picture of social practices and relations of power which were designed to assuage conflict and produce an efficient and enduring agency. The superior status of some members and a shared epiphany negated diversity. The differences between professions which would be expected to produce a holistic picture of the child were eroded, and consequently, alternative and potentially fruitful ways of understanding users were lost.

A common criticism of assessments of need is that they are governed by the availability of resources. There is evidence here of the crucial importance of direct access to a resource. The drive to manage risk is so important that it may never be possible to achieve purely 'needs based' purchasing.

There are considerable impediments at local levels to the integration of services for children in need. It is a contemporary 'wicked issue' (Edwards in Hodgkin and Newell, 1996, p.32). The needs of children cannot be tackled by one agency alone, and yet there are significant obstructions to disciplines and agencies working together. Studying the cloistered world of the 'clinic' asking what is gained and what is lost by the tactics of professionals produced some mechanisms for unlocking resistances to integration. It also generated a vision for welfare services for children and young people in the new century, and a conviction that children and their carers should be able to gain access to the whole range of provision by opening one 'virtual door'. The vital improvements to the environment in which children grow up in the UK will require the declaration of a 'state of emergency' in order to energise change.

I hope that the book is a good read. Chapter I necessarily provides the basis for all that follows. It shows how written products are windows into professional domains. The texts illustrate the findings and provide an interesting history of the child mental health agency. It will be gratifying if the general lessons about professional activity are used to improve services for children.

Chapter I
USING TEXT TO ANALYSE DECISION MAKING

Charlotte is a very unhappy child who has had a bad time during the last five years as a result of marital breakdown and changes of carer. She is one of an increasing band of children suffering from the breakdown of their parents' marriage, and where there has not been an effective and caring solution offered by either parent. At present the home situation is breaking down very rapidly and unpleasantly for her, and she is being scapegoated. She is playing into this situation by extremely disturbed and unpleasant behaviour at home. (Psychiatrist)

Child mental health services have developed in an unplanned, uncoordinated and 'historically determined' manner (NHS/HAS, 1995). Sometimes the National Health Service (NHS) provided them, sometimes Education Departments. The agency studied here came under the umbrella of a county council (Tradmore), although the workers were employed by their respective agencies (National Health Service and local education authority or Social Services). The following map sets the CAMHT and its residential resources on the landscape with other local agencies for children and families.

Between 1977 and 1988 approximately three thousand children were seen at 'the clinic'. One hundred and thirty-six of those children were placed in a residential unit. This 'hostel' provided termly care and support to the children whilst they attended local state schools. The outcomes for the children appeared to be good and my initial research proposal aimed to evaluate this hostel and contribute to the sparse literature on emotional disturbance in adolescent girls. Direct observation in the clinic and hostel was not permitted, but the agencies were willing to make the case records available (Gilbert, 1993). The records concerning the twenty-one pre-pubertal boys who were admitted during the decade were set aside and some records were missing. This left ninety-nine case files concerning girls for study.

Documents suffuse human service organisations (Plummer, 1983), and are a rich source of information about professional work. So, the detailed reading of records offers a route into

Figure I.1: *An Agency Map*

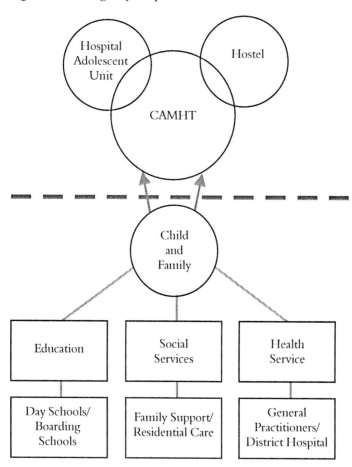

apparently 'impenetrable' social worlds (Silverman, 1993). This chapter introduces the CAMHT through examples of the different types of written material it produced. Some key themes created by the author's reading begin to emerge, particularly about the relations of power in the system.

There were two broad types of recording. 'Colloquial' writing which quickly removed the clinical facade because it was surprisingly passionate, and actively conveyed real people in dreadful situations, palpable pain, and exhibiting troubling behaviours:

> *Periods of high elation (at school) when charming and full of humour ... very deep gloom. Connie (14.2) makes funny noises ... walking into other pupils slouching against walls, loud shouting, set off fire alarms. Quick tempered. Fights. Drops bags out of windows. She can never explain why, deeply ashamed of her behaviour, worried about shaming her parents. Mother says always difficult at home. Father and she clash at times. Gentle persuasion and bullying get the best out of her. Connie feels she must be going mad and doesn't know why she does things. (Psychiatrist)*

'Scientific' writing was also persuasive and mostly left the reader in no doubt that something must be done:

> *Kim (11.10) was rather odd and infantile in her responses and showed some perseveration and stereotype in her behaviour. The possibility of early psychosis cannot be excluded, but in view of this sudden change, I think we ought to exclude any progressive intracranial lesion. (Psychiatrist)*

The challenge of introducing a more reflective, less action-driven culture into organisations working with risky and complicated situations became another dominant theme that is explored throughout the book. Introducing pauses will be difficult in the face of the convictedness of workers, that, for example, girls who 'scream uncontrollably' have needs that must be addressed urgently.

A Way of Reading

Exclusive membership of specialist communities is generally gained if members share:

1. A mutuality of history (Cicourel, 1987).
2. Familiarity with the organisation, procedure and culture.
3. Familiarity with clientele and authors (Garfinkel, 1967).
4. A shared frame of reference (Agar and Hobbs, 1982).

Acquiring a 'deep familiarity' (Lofland, 1995) with a social world requires the application of an open mind and a degree of irreverence to two types of reading:

'OVERVIEW' READING

This is scanning the field and observing the more obvious and rhetorical features of primary documents and records.

'CLOSE' READING

As my term implies, this is a more detailed dissection. The remainder of this chapter shares some of the outcomes of overview reading. Subsequent chapters are the products of close reading (Button, 1991). The method is straightforward despite the somewhat daunting theoretical basis (Hammersley and Atkinson, 1989). In essence it is a discourse analysis (Potter and Wetherall, 1987) using a combination of fracturing text (deconstruction), gathering facts, comparing and contrasting the data, and speculating on the effect of what is written (Taylor, 1996). In practice, the reader steps backwards and forwards into the text, both reading to make it strange and striving for a transparency (Strauss, 1987) about 'the everyday procedures that people use to make sense and order in (their) social world' (Parker, 1989, p.3). The foreigner is exploring the strategies and tactics used by actors (glossary), their interactions and the outcomes (Foucault, 1980).

Index cards captured ideas, headings, and buzzwords. These were sorted and resorted (Strauss, 1987), grouped and compared (Fielding, 1993). Some categories and groupings gained credibility and importance as the process continued. Links, patterns, and central themes crystallised. At the same time, many 'jottings in the margins' (Gherardi and Turner, 1987), were discarded because of the volume of material and ideas produced (Garnham and Oakhill, 1992).

'Overview' Reading

Case recording is a feature of the professional identity of social work and psychiatry (Pithouse, 1987). Both professions are essentially proprietorial about their products, therefore putting their records between the folders of the same clinic case file was highly symbolic. It proved fascinating to explore the form of collaboration and 'relations of power' (Clegg, 1989) that it represented.

From the 1930s to the 1970s CAMHSs were delivered by a tripartite of Child and Adolescent Psychiatrist, Psychiatric Social Worker, and Educational Psychologist or Child Psychotherapist (Sampson, 1980). They claimed that this combination provided a 'multidisciplinary assessment and treatment package for emotionally and behaviourally disturbed children' (Daines, 1985). Just glancing into the folders that contained the case records, drew this into question. Despite documents inside headed TRADMORE COUNTY COUNCIL, the local authority did not control the agency. Following the appointment of a 'Medical Director' in the 1960s, the case records were assumed to be the property of the health service. Case responsibility rested with consultant psychiatrists, and medical confidentiality restricted access to clinic workers only. The files were unwieldy, disorganised and frequently almost illegible. This provoked many questions about the quality and effectiveness of 'information sharing', and generated clusters of index cards in the coding and categorising process (Strauss, 1987). Perhaps the case files played little part in the endeavour, and merely represented a 'record of a therapeutic contract between the clinic, as a medico-legal enterprise, and the patient' as Garfinkel (1967, p.198) concluded.

Even at this early point, two factors – the dominance of medicine and medical etiquette, and the way the group work together – are gaining prominence in the performance evaluation.

Incoming Work

I should be grateful if you would investigate the problems of this family. When you have completed your advice … (Solicitor for the child in legal proceedings)

To explore the reception and immediate response to work, the records were subdivided into 'seeking advice'/'making a referral'/'responding/outlining actions' and so on, in order to follow the transitions. The referral process is explored in detail in Chapter II because it is such a crucial aspect of business and a neglected location for redistributing work between agencies.

This early foray into the written product shows how private transactions can be accessible to external appraisal:

> *I have been asked to assess with a view to giving a report to the Guardian ad litem (see glossary). I was asked to offer some advice about an appropriate plan for Sonia's future care, education, and treatment. (Psychiatrist)*

'Advice' implies giving an assessment to the referrer for them to progress. Yet as the next extract shows, the CAMHT assessor immediately proposed in-house service provision:

> *We should try to maintain family links (whilst providing) family therapy ... individual psychotherapy ... supportive residential placement which would enable us to achieve these objectives over the next two years ... (Psychiatrist)*

Advice was presented in a way that made an irresistible bid to keep the business. This demonstrates that language is not a neutral medium for information transfer, but a form of social action (Atkinson, 1990).

> *One favoured option would be for her to be placed at our hostel ... I would be happy to supervise and coordinate ongoing treatment for Sonia and her family. (Psychiatrist)*

At this point another broad theme about 'gatekeeping processes' has appeared, and will be revisited in Chapter VIII. An easy way to absorb the problem adds further irresistibility.

Identifying Needs and Allocating Services

Some professionals are warranted to make official declarations of 'need' (Woofit, 1993, NHS and Community Care Act, 1991, Children Act, 1989) and to allocate resources. Betty (13.3) had:

> *Peculiar attacks at school ... behaviour and speech almost psychotic ... overdose ... This unfortunate girl has been bereaved twice, first father then stepfather. She is the youngest and least intelligent of a very able and intellectual family and has found the going difficult. (Psychiatrist)*

They select particular 'data' from which to draw inferences:

> *I think (Betty's) acute psychotic breakdown was related to stress at school and an unusual form of epilepsy ... She is babyish in behaviour and speech. In response to stresses she can be a challenging and well-adjusted child. (Psychiatrist)*

A 'passport to services' is donated:

> *We feel she would do better in the hostel where she would have a stable environment among friendly people and at the same time would attend a socially less demanding school. (Psychiatrist)*

In this case, 'psychosis' had become a fact. The text was crafted to convince the reader that the new service was justified. Yet it also suppresses questions about whether other methods or agents could meet the identified needs. Is it possible to be 'psychotic' part of the time? Could the situation at school be modified? Such pondering underpins the argument developed in subsequent chapters, that there is much to be gained from exploring the assessment at these points. This formed the basis for the model of decision making presented in Chapter IX.

Audit

Garfinkel (1967) regarded case records as 'tokens' that business had been done. He subdivided them into 'actuarial' and 'contractual' functions.

> *We have already had two very fruitful case discussions which have led to*
> *increasing understanding of the complexity of the problem (Sonia), but*
> *have also led to clear thinking about possible solutions. (Psychiatrist)*

Actuarial text can help to enumerate the work of the organisation. In this extract, activity away from the work base, 'two meetings', and interagency contacts can be audited. This text is also contractual, showing work undertaken by employees. A theme emerged from the overview about the management and accountability of staff. The 'secondment' of social workers employed by the local authority Social Services Department (SSD) to the CAMHT produced a muddle about employee relations which was skilfully exploited. Psychiatric social workers could hide from their line managers behind the 'clinical accountability' of psychiatrists. Consequently, these employees were unmanaged, and seemingly, unmanageable. In the mid-nineties many Social Services Departments have, unwittingly, resolved this inability to govern an arms length workforce by withdrawing their staff from CAMHSs as a cost-saving exercise (NHS/HAS, 1995).

Internal Communications

Tracking 'communication with colleagues' was illuminating. Each discipline placed separate documents (detailed later) within the case record folder. The one exception was psychotherapy. Those records were not accessible to anyone. Reviewing the utility of records in the CAMHT could liberate authors from habitual, but apparently pointless, writing (Prince, 1996), because, in most cases, the sheer volume of written record was too great to be read by practitioners. The absence of a single, running, record indicated that there could be little cross-referencing. So, the design of the records provided early clues that claims about the efficacy of multidisciplinary working were overextended. In the main, each professional was working alone or at most with one other. The 'weekly case conference' which was trumpeted as a 'special feature' of the agency, was not a compensatory instrument because, due to time constraints, no more than a minority of cases could be discussed.

Facts and Opinions

> The actual events are not facts. It is the use of proper procedure for categorising events which transforms them into facts. A fact is something which is already categorised, which is already worked up so that it conforms to the model of what the fact should be like.
>
> Smith, 1978, p.35

The clinical record is intended to support, with 'firm evidence, the opinions and conclusions' of the author (King and Trowell, 1992, p.36). Surprisingly, in a 'professional' world, there appeared to be an abundance of supposition, speculation, musing and hypothesis (Schon, 1991).

> *An immature little waif (Alex) smokes twenty cigarettes … Wrote a note not conclusive of sexual abuse … Is not wanted … Marriage failing … Parental violence … Sees father occasionally … Happy at school … Very serious conduct disorder as a result of something quite abnormal in her upbringing … Deprived, neglected, some attachment to mother. The peak of her antisocial behaviour was when mother was abroad. (Psychiatrist)*

The challenge is to make professional work transparent because hypotheses are dangerous when seeded about amongst fact (Chapter V). They act to reinforce unproven matters, and confuse casework analysis (DHSS, 1985). If influential sections are broken down in an enquiring, if provocative, way into 'fact' and 'opinion', then apparent suppositions and issues that appear to be neglected can be discussed. This activity could produce a quantum leap in opportunity for the inquisition of professionals and introduce shifts in the relations of power, particularly in favour of users and

9

evaluators. It could also be used to value professional judgement. In the meantime, 'something' which the assessor cannot detect in Alex's 'upbringing' has disturbed her.

Summary

Textual analysis is dynamic, provocative and capable of extracting performance matters from difficult, resistive spaces. The method has already drawn attention to the history of an agency, the organisational structure, the distribution of power, the readership of records and gatekeeping. It has raised questions about the process and content of casework. Why were requests for advice not responded to with advice? Most importantly, the method can produce empirical material to inform current welfare debates, some of which are touched on in later chapters.

The next section shows how the 'overview' can expose even more obscure or subtle features.

A 'Dominant' Text

The typography and composition of documents and rules about inscription and distribution are rhetorical features of text which influence what actor may speak, what is spoken, and what is permitted to count. Such observations provoke ideas about the cultural ensemble and the location of actors. Monopolising voices are relatively easy to identify, and in the empirical world belonged to the child and adolescent psychiatrists.

Dominant documents act as 'charters' and propaganda for the agency. They reflect and support the organisational structure and prescribe processes of interaction. They are of major political importance and may, as in this example, suppress competition. Dominant text in other human service organisations may be in locations other than the case file, but here, ninety-five per cent of files contained a document entitled: 'CONFIDENTIAL PSYCHIATRIC AND SOCIAL HISTORY'.

The rubric of this ubiquitous, well-crafted, twelve-page booklet was compelling and prideful. High gains in status accompanied the medical lexicon. The title prepared the reader for a formal exhibit of professional activity and offered a powerful challenge to any doubters. This was reinforced by the caveat of confidentiality that invited the reader to become part of a privileged audience. The title validated agency involvement by indicating that the special combination of a 'psychiatric and social' perspective would be provided. The familiar tensions in mental health care around mental and social approaches to the analysis of situations (Totman, 1979) would appear to be addressed. As will be shown in the final part of this chapter, this was portrayed in an unsatisfactory way.

Typographical features including pre-printed headings and subheadings like 'Present Complaint(s), History of Complaints' and 'Symptoms' were useful evaluation tools because they encapsulated the discourse (Agar and Hobbs, 1982). Sections like 'Present State' contained subheadings: 'appetite, pica, anorexia, no breakfast'. Swings from technical to colloquial language again hinted at tensions in the discourse. Some of the headings were redundant, for example, no entries were made beside 'use of utensils' or 'care of dress'. Importantly, the language of 'Separations and Emotional Traumata,' 'Elimination' and so on prepared the reader for a theoretical orientation in which the child and the family, were 'patients' (Illich, 1978).

The 'Family History' section gathered information about 'emotional state' and 'psychiatric ill health'. There was interest in whether mother had a 'happy childhood' a question not posed to fathers. This was an early indication of the important position accorded to mothers (Bowlby, 1973), and a clue to a value system with an outdated picture of family life and parental responsibilities (pursued in more detail in Chapter III).

The tightly designed document was persuasive even before anything had been written on it. (A few documents on plain paper demonstrated the faint but unrepresentative presence of a different psychiatric method within the agency). The format implied that 'facts' were collected in a routinised manner. The notion of inaccuracy of some of the matters that were commented upon was easy to lose sight of: for example, recollection of when a child, now in her teens, began to 'babble' (Chess and Thomas, 1984).

The document culminated in a section headed 'Diagnosis'. Most actions germinated from this point. By implication, scientific reasoning has produced a precise answer (Gilbert and Mulkay, 1984). Instructions in the form of a 'Plan' were issued to other team members: 'Get School Report. Psychological Assessment. Full Social Work Report.'

Teasing out the components of these social constructions (Berger and Luckman, 1966) introduced the possibility of outcomes other than placement in residential care (Chapter V).

A Picture of Assessment Practices?

Headings organise and constrain the performer. In a sense they are oppressive because they dictate the content of work. Talk about 'Milestones' was not talk about aspects of contemporary daily life. In its favour, such detailed information gathering might defuse highly emotionally charged encounters (Dingwall, 1980).

The overview has raised questions about the contemporary efficacy of the dominant assessment method.

Blocks to External Appraisal

> Scientific reasoners seem to be peculiarly able to construct accounts in which they appear to have privileged access to the realities of the natural world.
>
> Gilbert and Mulkay, 1984, p.89

Delving in text made some of the process and content of a psychiatric consultation available for external appraisal. This is despite the tricks of textual governance like gaps and omissions, near illegibility and the 'secret code' of specialist terminology. Equally, the handwritten entries returned a sense of idiosyncrasy and vulnerability to what previously appeared to be a controlled process.

Rivals

Some text with rhetorical features of at least equal strength to the booklet was produced by educational psychology (Cline, 1980). In contrast to the psychiatric practice of 'mining' facts from interviews, this actor administered an armoury of tests.

> *To assess Jasmine's (14.3) dominant personality characteristics, the high school personality questionnaire was administered. (Educational Psychologist)*

This 'competitor' text was highly 'scientific' as in this description of Mary (13.3) who had been 'stealing from shops, and disruptive in school':

> *This (verbal performance) is statistically significant … One explanation for the discrepancy would be environmental privation. Indeed some authors suggest … It is also true might indicate some sort of specific cognitive deficit.*
>
> Psychometric Assessment
Weschler Intelligence Scale for Children – Revised Interpretation
(Educational Psychologist)

Megan (12.1) who had experienced 'severe marital conflict', was tested with the 'PA Inventory':

> *Personal Inferiority = low,*
> *Social Adjustment = high,*
> *Family Maladjustment = high,*
> *Daydreaming = low.*
> *The test shows a very disturbed young lady in Social and Family Maladjustment.*
>
> (Educational Psychologist)

Two features were striking about these products. First this actor could arrive at the same 'findings', and second, produce similar 'humanistic' text, as psychiatry:

She would like to be more loved by mother and father. She wishes she could comply with stepmother's wishes but finds it difficult … She feels rejected by both parents and is almost asking them to reject her further to prove her self-concept is true. Residential care seems best to both. (Educational Psychologist)

Some regulations determined which actor was warranted to produce the final assessment:

The parents seem inflexible in their attitude to her. Considering the amount of help they have received over the past eight years, they have changed very little. I am referring to the family psychiatric service and will look at the possibility of boarding education if they feel it appropriate. (Educational Psychologist)

Trying to understand how an educational psychologist could turn away from matters to do with school, drew attention to the powerful effect of shared belief systems. Gail (11.8):

… Had some school refusal problems at primary school but these resolved without too much difficulty. She transferred to secondary school satisfactorily until after a few weeks she was asked to move class to help a friend who was upset. She now says this move upset her. Gail is not anxious, bar a frequent need to go to the toilet. A sensitive child who may be overreacting to minor problems especially in relation to peers.

Gail has been very obstinate, resisting all attempts by school, myself and her parents to get to school. Last term the home tutor tried to set up a desensitisation approach, but she refused to go in the car. (Educational Psychologist)

The possibility of working on the problems with peers was overwhelmed by the predominant interest of the agency in the emotional world of the child.

The Pickford Projective Pictures Test: Gail is unable to see the possibility of change within herself. The correlation between her ideal self and the real self is very high and this perhaps suggests that she is clinging to the hope that she will be able to avoid anxiety-

provoking situations by maintaining her present behaviour. (Educational Psychologist)

So a diffident and sensitive personality was featured:

Friendships are tremendously important. She is oversensitive to the comments and behaviours of peers. She may now feel she has lost so much face that she cannot confront her friends again. In all situations she expressed fear of physical injury to herself and others. This may express her general anxiety about life. (Educational Psychologist)

The final phrase reinforced the bid for transfer of case responsibility to the psychiatrist. (A way of mapping this process is illustrated in Appendix I, and discussed in Chapter IV):

Her parents say that she has threatened to kill herself several times.

But maintained an affinity between education and psychiatry:

Psychiatric assessment perhaps to be carried out whilst she has a temporary bed at the hostel. (Educational Psychologist)

Educational psychology could have been the dominant voice, and indeed it was in some child guidance clinics. However, in order to avoid rivalry and retain an ecological niche in this agency, this actor put self-imposed limits on their services, exploited a linkage in discourses and conformed. In the nineties educational psychology separated itself from the CAMHT and regained power through independence. It would be wise in any service evaluation to pay attention to how power differentials are negotiated.

Subordinates

Psychiatric Social Workers (PSWs) produced copious records (Lask and Lask, 1981). In contrast with their peers in the Social Services teams whose attention was directed to the child, their primary duties were to the parent(s). Children fell strictly in the psychiatrist's domain. The consultant prescribed PSW involvement, sometimes grudgingly:

Even if a social history were available I think I would prefer to take my own. (Psychiatrist)

Taking the history was an important element of the art of capturing the problem. It reified and transformed it into a solid entity.

The Problem: described as 'anxiety symptoms' was one of intermittent stomach pains for which no organic explanation could be found. These started when Sally (13.4) began school at five years old. (Psychiatric Social Worker)

Generally, the 'social history' had headings which mimicked psychiatry: 'Present complaint, History of complaints, Early history, Present state, Family history.' The authors reiterated the psychiatrist's or the parents' viewpoint. In common with the educational psychologist, it was predicated on the belief that what happened in the past reverberated in the present:

Early history: no problems reported by parents, as a baby did not walk for fourteen months. (Psychiatric Social Worker)

Early feeding, weaning, age at walking and talking did not go unremarked. Sandra's (13.2) 'Early history' noted her birth weight and 'no difficulties at delivery'.

She was found to have a heart murmur. This led to admissions to (hospital). Anxious few months. Disruption in bonding for this early period. Breastfed for three weeks but because of difficulties mother gave up. Now regrets this. Feeding has never been something that Sally has been interested in. Never a cuddly baby unlike (sibling). She has always been small. Mother showed me pictures of Sally as a younger child, even then had rather a gaunt look.

Normal milestones.

Social Development: … outward going from nursery days.

Health: After the initial anxiety over the heart murmur, Sally has been remarkably healthy according to mother. (Psychiatric Social Worker)

PSWs collected but rarely analysed information even when it came fully within the purview of social work. For example, the many stressors (Coleman, 1990) that impinged on Nina (14.11):

> *Referred because of recent stealing and refusal to go to school. Just before her first birthday, (father) broke his back and became wheelchair bound. Two years later (he) divorced mother in order to remarry. Continued contact was enjoyed. Nina last met her father on her thirteenth birthday, and he died two months later. Two years after the divorce (mother) remarried and (paternal uncle came to live with the family). Mother found this very stressful because both treated her like a mother. (Her husband) had been raised in an orphanage, and the brother-in-law clung to her like a lovesick child. Neither man exerted authority over the children. (Father) escaped by going abroad to work. Mother had severe hepatitis and was expected to die (then) husband asked for a divorce ... Mother became diabetic ... (She) succeeded in getting brother-in-law out of the house ... Nina started to shoplift Sindy Doll toys. (The next month) mother had to wear a neck collar ... Positive smear test. With all these worries and her ageing mother to support mother turned to her daughter for support. (Psychiatric Social Worker)*

This offering to the psychiatrist did not attempt to promote different systems of ideas or an independent perspective. These workers had a language for analysis but chose not to use it. Childcare practitioners located in Social Services Departments are also poor at evaluating information (DH, DEE, HO, 2000). The evidence suggests that these shortfalls originate in relations of power as much as in shortfalls in training. Social work had assumed the role of assistant, acolyte or nurse. In practice, little interest was shown in the social work history, and their work with carers appeared undervalued.

> *There has been very considerable improvement since my discussions (two meetings) with (Jane's) family. Unfortunately, it is very difficult for the family to attend for ongoing supportive sessions, and we have accepted second best for our psychiatric social worker to visit stepmother at home. (Psychiatrist)*

Suppressing Difference

The loss of 'difference' is an important analytical theme, which is explored in detail in Chapter IV. Macdonald (1977), found that social workers and psychiatrists produced different accounts and interpretations of the same situation. This could be observed in the empirical world. For example, the psychiatric social worker composed a very clear account of the many dislocations in Rhian's life, and concluded:

> *The last three years have seen the dispersal of her family, the loss of her substitute home, continuing covert conflict between parents, and restricted access to her father with whom she has an affectionate bond.*

However, these 'alternative' perspectives were lost as bridges were constructed to the psychiatric account:

Two main tasks:

1. *Treat her anorexia.*
2. *Make some sense of her social situation. (Psychiatric Social Worker)*

And then this was reinforced by tapping into an in-house prescription:

> *She would appear to need stable care away from home. (Psychiatric Social Worker)*

Rhian was admitted to the adolescent unit for treatment of 'anorexia'. In that environment, social factors re-emerged:

> *She has said a great deal about her unhappy domestic situation. (Psychiatrist)*

This was greeted as a new finding:

> *I hope we will be able to get to the bottom of her problem quickly. (Psychiatrist)*

These processes severely restricted the scope for alternative ways of construing situations. This performance issue is returned too frequently.

Summary

Psychiatric Social Workers undertook 'constructional maintenance' tasks for the team. They melded the multidisciplinary group together by pairing up with a Psychiatrist, Psychotherapist or Psychologist. They sustained a symbiotic relationship with that dominant actor by continually reinforcing the psychiatric perspective and allowing them to be responsible for standards of practice. This coalescence produced a gain in status and weakened lines of accountability. The social worker has emerged from this analysis as a component of the prescription like tablets, someone to absorb the angst of carers and so facilitate the work between the Psychiatrist and the child. Their dependability and the consistent support that they invested in mothers were quite remarkable. The limited difference they imposed on the psychiatric reality in this agency in the late twentieth century is striking, particularly given the influence the profession had in the early development of clinics. Reinforcing the dogma was a form of rational accountancy designed as a survival mechanism by an increasingly marginalised discipline. In the nineties many social work posts in CAMHTs were withdrawn. This was the right move, but cost saving was the wrong reason. Severance was justified because social workers did not bring a different social work perspective to bear on the work of the clinic. The evidence here suggests that their reintroduction and subsequent role definition and management should ensure that they provide a social work perspective on the child and their world. Whatever professions team members in tiers one to four are in (NHS, 1995), managers and supervisors must strive to maintain 'difference'.

Social work has evolved a capacity to adapt and clone in different working environments (Jones 1991, Pithouse, 1987). Adaptation is an excellent survival tactic in an ever changing culture, but any profession is weakened if it does not carry with it rights to a 'space' of its own. The language used to describe the knowledge, theory and practice can claim these rights, which contribute to a particular expertise.

Conclusion

So far the research method has produced:

1. A picture of the role and function of an organisation.
2. An introduction to how teams interact.
3. Commentary on the efficiency and effectiveness of the Service.
4. Many ideas to pursue.

It has begun to show some conditions which suppress difference in multidisciplinary teams that have certain characteristics:

a. Where the definitive social construction rests with one party.
b. When the relationships of power are hierarchical.
c. When the disciplines form close-working dyads or triads.
d. When the interdisciplinary cultural ensemble has vested interests in survival.
e. When one party is dependent on another for work.

Text in this social world is a map without place names. This is a strategy to ward off intruders. A crude classification of documents and records has provided some boundaries, and the 'reading' method has provided directions and a compass so that the uninitiated can gain access and examine the social and political functions of the domain.

The chapter has also introduced the ethnographic world. Already there is an impression of a tyranny so powerful that, by the end of the century, two professions withdrew from the agency and avoided suffocation. It is also possible to see how children may not, be able as objects of mental disorder, to influence their situation, and nor could other associated actors. Finally, significant themes are beginning to emerge from the reading:

- At any point in time several ways of looking at the situation can be found in the records.
- Points of significant change for the client are clearly visible in the record.

The products of 'close' reading are presented through the ensuing chapters, beginning with detailed analysis of the reception of work.

Chapter II
INITIAL TEXT

Sally (14.4) has been a great trial and problem to her parents (and) appears to be subject to intermittent episodes of violent behaviour aimed at her parents, who find it impossible to control her (and) are incapable of coping … and have little insight into the problem. I would be grateful for any help and advice you can give. (Family Medical Practitioner)

This chapter describes tactics used in referral making. Even at the beginning of a case management sequence there is evidence that inadequacies in professional performance and access to a particular resource influence activity. Referral routes are neither 'fickle' (Millham, 1978), nor 'at least to some extent a matter of chance' (Cliffe and Berridge, 1991, p.209). The only random factor is the choice of referrer.

The disposal of cases is not driven purely by the needs of clients. Common influences upon referrers were found to be:

- The failure of previous interventions.
- Risk levels.
- An idea about an appropriate resource.
- A value system.
- Acquaintance with the recipient agency.
- An ability to match eligibility criteria.
- The system of social relations in which the referrer is embedded.
- Custom and practice.

A Waymarked Path

Referrers have to break through agency defences. In the CAMHT these were constructed to avoid unplanned contact with families or non-medical referrers.

> *I (Head Teacher) have made repeated attempts to contact you (Psychiatrist) and finally got your secretary to whom I explained the urgency of the problem.*

At school Kim was 'bullying and terrorising and can only be contained for short periods'. The 'earliest possible appointment' was sixteen days later. These typical timescales took little account of the situations for fieldworkers. Irritation led to protest about the inaccessibility of the service, particularly from Social Services. For a short while, in the mid-eighties, agencies other than medicine could refer directly. Overall eighty-five per cent of requests for help were from health professionals:

> *I have been seeing Lotte for the past few months for obesity ... She has lost two stone ... Very sensitive to teasing ... Family need help in her management. She has now been refusing school all this term. (General Practitioner)*

In letters requesting 'assessment', or 'advice about the management of this very difficult girl', referrers calibrated their appeal to 'fit' the services (Bosk, 1988). References to 'intermittent episodes ... violence ... insight' are designed to interest one agency and exclude others (Huczymski and Buchanan, 1991). Limited information shaped the situation, and in general reinforced but added little to the parental narrative. Jo's (12.1) behaviour appeared inappropriate for a girl verging on adolescence:

> *Neurotic ... morose won't go to school ... Seen by her parents as ill ... selfish and (subject to) temper tantrums. (General Practitioner)*

Mixing medical information, family matters, and unmanageable child behaviour, produced an irresistible dish.

Referrers were apparently searching for two things:

EXPLANATIONS

> *Firstly, your views on the underlying reasons for Sonia's (14.5) stated rejection of her adoptive family … Is this simply adolescent rebellion, … failure of parental management … an adoption issue or is it possible that the problems have arisen from something inherent in Sonia's personality? (Solicitor for the child in legal proceedings)*

ADVICE

> *Your advice on the best way of managing the present crisis in the relationship would be valued. There is the question of a proper care plan and educational placement … Is it possible that a school which combines a high standard of education with a psychotherapeutic function might better meet her needs? If so are you able to suggest any such establishment? (Guardian ad litem)*

A contrasting genre of letters (five per cent) came from community social workers. The prose was fluid, generous in family detail, and less concentrated on the child. Authors expressed frankly their ignorance and curiosity, and made bids for support in their casework:

> *The girls accuse the mother of getting father into florid outbursts. It is almost as though Lindsay (14.10) has to draw attention to herself to stop arousing father. There is a family secret here which I feel needs to be handled, but I am at a loss to know how to make a beginning perhaps (the psychiatrist) has ideas? (Community Social Worker)*

Occasionally general practitioners helped to circumvent the rules on behalf of other agencies, as here where the family doctor composed a letter on behalf of Social Services:

> *Making vague suicide threats … unhappy at school … Recently bereaved of her mother. A school friend has disappeared. (General Practitioner)*

Compliance with the etiquette was rewarded:

> *I think she is well enough to cope with school .... The approach should be matter of fact and encouraging rather than trying to get her to talk. Her management is better left to us at the clinic because I think this will be rather an intensive business which will require careful monitoring. (Psychiatrist)*

The General Practitioner and the Community Social Worker were required to withdraw. It was widely accepted that the CAMHT did not form inclusive working relationships:

> *It would be disadvantageous for both of us to be working independently on the case. Please let me know if support and treatment is being offered. If not, we will resume the case. (Psychiatric Social Worker to Psychiatrist)*

Those excluded from co-work resented requests to pick up cases that were subsequently discarded or where families did not cooperate. This is a Psychiatric Social Worker's note of a conversation with a Community Social Worker:

> *Criticised the child guidance team saying they 'ought to be working with the family to re-establish Margaret (11.3) back home'. I tried unsuccessfully to explain that Margaret's mother could not be worked with. That (Margaret) was far too disturbed, and parents were not prepared to work in a family therapy situation. To this (the community social worker) responded: 'I don't see why we should be dumped with an unsatisfactory problem'. I said I would make a note of the statement, and the conversation ended inconclusively. (Community Social Worker)*

Arbiters of Normality

Children who were stealing, displaying a temper, soiling, complaining of aches and pains, or not going to school were directed to the clinic. Nichola (8.7) was 'moody ... weeps a lot ... sleeps poorly ... and is being difficult about getting to school'.

Nina needed 'counselling (about the death of her father), and control, but she can accept neither'. A mass of disciplinary issues accompanied Sally (see also introductory quotation):

> *Out of parents' control, temper tantrums ... accused brother-in-law of sexual advances ... Sally attacked mother ... Full of aggression, when little used to smack the bottoms of old ladies in shops. Wants to be slim ... faddy ... drinks, smokes, swears ... blackmailing ... wrecks father's papers ... steals from mother ... shoplifts – an extremely disturbed girl throughout her childhood. (Psychiatrist)*

Behaviour was made strange, and 'doctor's orders' coerced the parents of a shy and bullied child to accept clinic services:

> *Joy (12.7) has had difficulty making friends since she was young. Has one friend who is about to move away ... Is quiet and withdrawn at school. (Two weeks ago) she said girls were bullying and she hid (instead of going to school). Now she is refusing to go despite mother's attempts to escort her ... when she was little she cried a lot and was clingy. She has a feeling that no one likes her. (Psychiatrist)*

It is apparent from the referral letters that this universe was closely engaged in the social regulation of children (Chapter VI). Laura (14.8) who was suffering from 'adolescent psychosis' was extremely challenging. In school she:

> *Giggled to herself ... (ostracised) threw a tomato in science. Said it had been thrown at her ... Said it was the devil in her. Attention seeking. Odd facile expressions, vacant smile, non-person. (Psychiatrist)*

There were only five cases of frank mental illness. The majority of referrals were about 'odd', 'neurotic' or delinquent children.

Value Driven Activity

In the absence of consistently applied thresholds and gatekeeping mechanisms, referral routes are strongly influenced by personal attitudes and beliefs. The poor quality of the care system and class prejudice undoubtedly influenced decisions. Consequently, at a conservative estimate, fifteen per cent of these referrals were wholly inappropriate. This group of 'severely deprived' children needed referral to a Social Services Department:

> *Fiona (13.7) had a bedroom in a garden shed next to an outside lavatory. The relationship between the child and her stepmother has been deteriorating over four years … Parents totally rejecting. Fiona refuses this but would prefer to stay at home. No evidence of difficult or provocative behaviour. A pleasant, articulate girl who wonders if her parents love her. Parents are asking for foster parents and all links to be severed. (General Practitioner)*

Annabelle's (15.2) parents complained to their doctor that she was:

> *Disobedient, rude and defiant … taken twenty pounds from a relative. Caught trying to put a lighted match in a car petrol tank. Third child of six … often took her sibling's belongings, not washing properly, smoking, buying pornographic material. Getting into a lot of trouble at school. (General Practitioner)*

An external child psychiatrist said Jasmine's boarding school placement had 'broken down'. Jasmine was moved to a Social Services Observation and Assessment Centre (O and A):

> *A pleasant girl who related extremely badly to her parents. Mother has given up on her. Her stepfather did not want her to escape from the (O and A) and 'get into more trouble'. He saw her as 'embarrassing'. Her problems are multiple. She is of average intelligence but expected to achieve more by school. She also has an unrealistic idea of her ability. In the past Jasmine has persistently stolen from school and family. She has had the developmental problems of enuresis and encopresis. (Referring Psychiatrist)*

In the absence of gatekeeping mechanisms, the signs of positive change were not weighed against the costs of transfer to the hostel (not least because it closed in the school holidays):

> *Encopresis continued until admission but has now abated. At (the O and A) Jasmine is settling and functioning reasonably well. I become more and more convinced that this girl should not stay with her parents. I feel she needs ongoing psychiatric treatment but could manage normal school. Short contact with her parents would be reasonable, but a full summer home would lead to difficulties. (Referring Psychiatrist)*

Even at this early point, the powerful way that words construct and limit the picture of a young person's world is clear:

> *I think many of her problems relate to the very difficult home circumstances. She is fostered.*

Any sense that children's reactions to family situations were normal disappeared as information that was interesting to the agency was presented:

> *Foster mother has marked diabetes and is in danger of blindness. The eldest adopted son (adult) suffers from depression and obsessional disorders and requires a lot of psychiatric support. In many ways, she has started to copy him. (Psychiatrist)*

The pictures were awash with medical and psychiatric matters and multidimensional problems.

Choosing a CAMHT also avoided three sources of stigma (Chapters III and IX). Firstly, that associated with Social Services:

> *I do not want Social Services care because they have no facilities for looking after (Jasmine 14.10). Yet it sounds as if her mother has totally rejected her; one can only get her to focus on her daughter for five minutes. (Referring Psychiatrist)*

Secondly, the inevitable association between the 'bad' child and shortfalls in parenting was avoided if the child was 'ill' or 'mad' and needed 'adjustment'. Thirdly, female delinquency could occasion punishment rather than cure (Cain, 1991):

(Jasmine 14.10) has been a lifelong problem. Mother a hardbitten Scot – three husbands ... Soiler from age two to three. Steals – a symptom of neurotic disturbance not conduct disorder, although she is with a lot of children in that category ... been in residential school. They cannot contain her. At home manageable. Always presents herself as a sweet child but soon her disturbance shows through. (Referring Psychiatrist)

Risk Management

The continuing unmanageability of the child, coupled with carer's declarations that they were 'at the end of their tether ... unable to cope ... such a problem she should be taken away' places great pressure upon solo practitioners. Samantha (15.0) saw the General Practitioner, two months previously, complaining of:

Earaches, but no abnormality could be found (She had been sent home from school several times). I prescribed Impramine (antidepressant and sedative) at night. (General Practitioner)

Medication did not cure the symptoms. Referral was made to an Educational Psychologist, but a delayed response prompted a referral to CAMHT:

In the last two weeks there has been a steady deterioration. She has eaten little and looks unwell and unhappy ... She has had several hysterical outbursts at school ... Her parents have been to look at another school. (They are) desperate to know how to manage her. (General Practitioner)

As an 'insurance' against rebuttal the author concluded: 'I think she could be heading for anorexia'. Where one route is barred, the case holder uses another (Malek, 1991). The pressure arising from working in situations of risk, in the absence of effective therapies, was the most significant catalyst operating at this point. Julie's

(15.9) 'leg pain, hip pain, influenza, and tummy ache' persisted despite treatment over several months. The general practitioner painted a suitable portrait of a child with 'anxiety and depression ... minor illness ... and mother's agreement (to non-attendance at school)', who required psychiatric appraisal.

The importance of referral activity cannot be overstated. Quelling the rising sense of chaos was achieved by 'narrowing' the focus, magnifying the problems, and using medical language (Chapter V). The child had become an 'object' of concern, a 'patient with a problem'.

Conclusion

Exploring the politics of referral by unpacking that key point, has exposed influential factors. The language chosen creates and limits frameworks of expectation (Mehan, 1987). To cope with the tensions derived from the inadequacy of their interventions, the complexity of situations, the demands of clients, and delays and shortfalls in provision, an effective referrer conforms to protocols and speaks in a particular language. Unwittingly, referrers govern the nature of the long term as well as short-term outcomes for the child. Their preferences:

- Exclude a number of other helping agencies, and
- In this social world, affirmed the views of parents and others that something was 'wrong' with the child which was unconnected to their parenting style.

The long-term influence of this actor on the future of the service user justifies investment in the careful analysis of their work. The unregulated system in this research universe permitted an agency to have extensive, idiosyncratic influence over referrers. It dictated who could approach and how they should behave. The process allowed the individual social actor's values to become too significant. Detailed evaluation of referral processes can alter the distribution of work between agencies. This is increasingly important because devices like eligibility criteria are hardening the referral interface. When agencies alter criteria about incoming work, they would be wise to test the response of referrers. They may just learn a new language in order to circumvent the obstruction.

The child and family have now entered the world of the CAMHT. Performance analysis demands consideration of the philosophy and ethics that underpin an agency.

The next chapter paints some of that detail, and the impact it had on the ways consumers were served.

Chapter III
A MEDICINE OF BEHAVIOUR

Sandra's only chance as regards her development is to be removed from the family. She needs an opportunity to be respected as an individual with an identity, with acceptance and value. Given the right circumstances, she could function at a much better level. (Psychiatrist)

The moral order of a domain suffuses documents, casework records, mission statements, and the literature of the various disciplines. It has far-reaching effects on practice. This chapter describes some instrumental features in the CAMHT:

- An anticollectivist philosophy.
- A principle of 'voluntarism'.
- A 'rule of confidentiality'.

I have called the blend of dogma about children's development and mental health, adolescence, and females, a 'medicine of behaviour' (glossary)*. In combination these features made a major contribution to hiding the disciplinary role of the agency (Chapter VI), and to areas of inadequate performance.

Anticollectivism

Families are the social and psychological crucible within which each child's personality is shaped, and the foundation laid for subsequent competencies and problems.

Rappoport, 1987, p.35

---

* This is a reference to Foucaults' 'Medicine of Tissues', 1977.

Customers were enticed by a milieu that respected family privacy and was opposed to state intervention. The clinic was proud that it was a 'non-statutory' service. State services, in particular Social Services, were regarded as inferior because they encroached on individual freedoms, and fostered dependency (Rojek et al., 1988). Their workforce was regarded as inept, unsophisticated in their remedies, unable to cope with complexity, and prone to remove children into environments that were not 'safe and containing':

> *Small children's homes, in spite of the best efforts of the staff tend to have many limitations and present a bleak prospect for Sonia with her many talents. A sophisticated foster home that could handle her would be ideal, but such homes are very rare assets. (Guardian ad litem)*

Social Services were a last resort even in the obvious cases of total family breakdown. The CAMHT tried not to involve them.

> *It is in (Sonia's) interests to board away. Care would be seen by her as total rejection, and in the long term she would be damaged by it. (Psychiatrist)*

Clinic workers dissociated themselves from monopolistic and inefficient bureaucracies by accentuating their technical skills and their 'voluntary', rather than compulsory relationship with 'patients'. Social Services were avoided, even where they held statutory parental rights (Children and Young Persons Act, 1969):

> *I (Psychiatrist) thought I would drop you (GAL) a note following (a meeting with Social Services). I am concerned that some of the staff of the Social Services Department are taking a rigid stand which can only aggravate the difficulties in getting good parental cooperation … I would be concerned if Sonia were not getting some kind of supervision and support from outside the Social Services Department.*

Ultimately, this duo gained the support of the court to separate Sonia from the influence of her 'administrative parent' (Adcock and White, 1983), and she was placed at the hostel (Chapters V and X).

The idealisation of the family had two important consequences:

1. Inadequate exploration of family conflict; and
2. Maligning family members demanded considerable mental leaps.

A Principle of 'Voluntarism'

Without the force of law to protect children, the clinic was dependent on the motivation of its clients. This significantly influenced the way staff behaved and the assessment (Chapter IV). Psychiatric Social Workers were not encouraged to help people attend. Fear, class barriers, poverty, transport, and childcare arrangements were not their business (Jordan, 1990). Nor did the clinic insist that certain members of the family attend. They worked with whoever turned up, and consequently rarely saw siblings, fathers, and the wider family. This non-coercive relationship was used as test of the carer's commitment to their child, and a further distinction from 'statutory' agencies.

The logic was dangerous. Irresponsible, abusive parents would be involuntary attendees at Social Services (Parton, 1994). Parents attending the clinic of their own volition must be caring, concerned and harmless. Consequently, there was little interest in family interaction and parenting style. It also stopped staff challenging the volunteers, and, for example, insisting that parents become meaningfully involved in the work with their child. Not only would that be impolite, it might cause parents to withdraw. Indeed, analysis showed that the absence of strategies to manage non-compliance haunted the whole interaction.

A Rule of Confidentiality

A further factor that contributed to the production of a non-intrusive set of social relations was the rule about the privacy of the family and their information. This empowered parents, at the expense of children:

> *I have been given permission by (Sonia's (14.9) adoptive father) to use the information obtained during interviews for this report. (Psychiatrist's court report)*

Sonia's adoptive father, who it will be argued in Chapter VIII, was probably harming her, was in a very safe position.

> The cast iron assurance of confidentiality that clinics were able to offer encouraged patients to reveal aspects of themselves which could be of considerable value in the therapeutic process.
>
> King and Trowell, 1992, p.38

The CAMHT claimed to provide a 'private space where (children could) explore experiences and feelings with safety and confidence' (Psychotherapist). It was feared that without confidentiality the clinicians would lose control:

> The nature of the relationship is likely to change completely ... Patients may demand an explanation of information contained in a court report or will disagree with conclusions and recommendations reached. The views expressed may be so unacceptable that it becomes impossible to undertake any work with the family.
>
> Ibid., p.38

These rules served to:

1. Avoid challenges to the assessment.
2. Hide problems and conflicts in the family.
3. Exclude outside agencies.
4. Retain control of the case.

More obscure gains included:

a. A sound defence against challenge.
b. Protection of the discourse.
c. Sustained elitism.

However, these parents and children showed little sign of being able to use these secret places (Chapter VII). It became evident that for these children confidentiality and secrecy could not be supported (Ryan and Wilson, 1995). Secrecy suggests that difficulties in family life are 'unhealthy' rather than normal.

Theoretical Foundations

> It is, we believe, a recipe for disaster for professionals ever to become so enmeshed in a particular theory or approach that it becomes taken for granted.
>
> Stainton Rogers et al., 1989, p.50

The theoretical constructs referred to by the CAMHT were neither simple, nor simply put, and the language and a vast literature were a powerful tactic to exclude outsiders (Rutter and Hersov, 1985). Their talk was generally not about growth, change, experiments, mistakes, sexual abuse, puberty, or stress. The clinic rarely made the contemporary fragmentation, reconstitution (Wallerstein, 1988), and isolation of the family, the raising of the school leaving age, peer group influences, or poverty and unemployment, the central cause of stress.

> *Pat (15.5) used to soil and wet but this stopped since (father's third wife) cared for her. It seems she is very resentful of all mother figures and shows her aggression in her attitude to her stepmother. Father feels he must choose between daughter and wife ... There is an unhappy breakdown in family relationships, which is having an adverse effect on her adjustments everywhere. (Psychiatrist)*

Generally, it was vulnerabilities in personality and shortfalls in development (either acquired or inherited), which produced psychological disturbance (Early and Porter, 1993) and 'behaviour problems'.

> One of the most compelling and essential means of achieving warrant is through reference to mental events.
>
> Shotter and Gergen, 1989, p.74

Poor concentration, suicide gestures, running away, stealing, drug abuse, promiscuity, anger, depression, attention seeking and aggression were described as 'acting out' behaviours. These 'discharged emotions' arose from the child's 'pathological', 'disturbed' or 'maladjusted' nature. Thinking that the service provided the milieu in which children could share their problems, clinicians thought that those who did not speak out were disordered (Chapter VII). The theory of 'acting out' did not allow for mundane causes. Assessors appeared oblivious to children being stopped in their tracks by not being 'allowed to have pierced ears' or by their imperfections when compared with their peers:

> '*I (Jean 13.4) don't like being big. I want to be normal weight. I can't play games. I don't want to go to school or even outdoors until I lose weight.' (Psychologist)*

The concentration on 'symptoms' was striking, and contrasts with the idea that acting out is a 'cue for despair' (Chapter IX), and a substitute for crying (Coleman, 1987).

Missing School

There was a great deal of careful work to distinguish 'typical school phobia' (Lotte 13) from a 'typical school refusal' (Gail 12). However, on close reading, the clusters of symptoms and characteristics overlapped:

> *(Kate 14.3) School refusal associated with considerable emotional disturbance, anxiety and depression. (Psychologist)*

> *(Sheila 15.0) Intractable school phobia anxiety about puberty … anxiety about separating from mother. (Psychologist)*

How the terms were used was intriguing. Thirteen per cent of the cases attracted both terms. So Jackie's (12.1) 'very severe school phobia and depression' changed to 'school refusal, depression, and social isolation' when she was admitted to the adolescent psychiatric unit. In the literature 'school phobia' (thirty-four per cent of all the cases), 'school refusal' (fifty per cent) and 'truancy' (Rutter and Hersov, 1985) were connected with 'separation anxiety' (Bowlby, 1973), parental 'overprotectiveness', stress (Coleman, 1987), 'anxiety', and family dynamics (Bryce and Baird, 1986). There were tensions, even a tangle, and certainly no consensus about the explanation. Four uses were apparent:

1. Where each term was clearly defined;
2. Confused usage;
3. Terms used interchangeably;
4. Where one term 'school refusal' was used as a catch-all phrase.

To address this muddle, Bowlby (1977) had preferred this last term because 'it was the most descriptive and the least laden with theory'.

There were two clusters in the data, one of 'school phobic' children who had 'passive', 'collusive' and 'overprotective' parents, and were much younger than those in the second group. These were the 'refusers', who were more defiant and deviant as well as slightly less intelligent. The child appeared more active in school refusal and more passive in phobia. The choice of diagnostic term was closely related to the degree to which ownership of the case had to be justified. So 'truancy', that is absence without legitimate cause or parental permission, was rarely used because naughty and antisocial behaviour could readily become the business of other agencies. No effort was invested in typifying Debbie's (14.7) 'mild anxiety and few friends', beyond 'school avoidance', perhaps because there was no external agency involvement. The terms had tactical importance where there was competition for the work. A declaration of mental disturbance won the case:

> *Phobic Anxiety State, arising from separation anxiety, reinforced by lack of success in work and relationships at school. (Psychiatrist)*

Simplifying the language might have resulted in other agencies giving services or allowed other parties to disagree with the sense being made. It seems reasonable to suggest that the choice of terminology was tautological, and a strategy to exhibit 'professional' skill, and the continuing need for psychiatric services. Language is politically very powerful.

Separation Anxiety

The agency's residential 'hostel' was interesting because it offered voluntary shared care to families (Taylor, 1996). It seemed a very successful and palatable intervention (Chapter VIII), and of particular interest in the light of the philosophy of the Children Act 1989 (DH, 1989 (a) and (b)). Intriguingly, separation was a benign intervention when it was 'prescribed' in the form of a residential placement, but harmful when it occurred in family life:

> *Sonia (14.5) had rather uncertain and possibly inconsistent care up to the age of nine months when she was fostered. This type of inconsistent care is well known to render children vulnerable and to impair their ability to form attachments later on. (Psychiatric Social Worker)*

In her early months, Sonia oscillated between her mother and foster parents (depicted in Appendix II):

> *Further damage was done by Sonia having to leave after two months, so she was twelve months old before she was back in the care of (foster parents).*

These foster parents subsequently adopted her:

> *(Adoptive father) observed that when she returned she was superficially very pleased to see them, but he noticed what he described as a kind of blankness. The parents noticed that in her play she seldom played with dolls and seemed to prefer more serious and abstract pursuits (playing bookshops). (Psychiatrist)*

Early 'attachment' and 'separation' (Bowlby, 1973) experiences explained current behaviours:

> *These observations are unfortunately very typical of children who have had early infant deprivation. The outward ability to relate very quickly and superficially in a cheerful and jolly way, coupled with difficulty in making really deep attachments, is only too common in such children, and many with this experience would be particularly vulnerable to any further breakdown in relationships or separation. (Psychiatrist)*

Parental rejectiveness and family fragility harmed children.

> *(Ann) Very suitable for the hostel ... If stays at home in the present circumstances, it seems likely she will deteriorate and the family may break under the stress. If we could get her away for a while, we may be able to help her readjust to the stresses of the domestic background, while working with mother and stepfather so that she can eventually return home happily. (Psychiatrist)*

Assessors believed that separation and 'shared care' protected the child from psychological harm, and maintained their place in the family. They also arranged it for the children who were severely deprived and neglected:

> *The outlook without intervention is poor. The only hope is for her (Alex) to get away from home for at least part of the time at our hostel. (Psychiatrist)*

Removal from a harmful environment was 'the only chance (for Sandra) to minimise rejection' and the way to diffuse conflict in Ann's family:

> *Reports by mother and the Educational Psychologist show that a tense and critical situation has developed at home. It would be advantageous for both to have a period of temporary separation. Admitted to me that she has thought about running away. I cannot promise that an occasional outpatient appointment is likely to generate the peace and tolerance that is required for dealing with the girl's difficulty. (Psychiatrist)*

Shortfalls in the service provision, and here it might be the infrequency of appointments or a mutual reluctance to consider difficult and contentious issues at these points, were obscured by moving the child out of the family.

A Preventative Service

Prediction justified intervention:

I do not think that we should go on much longer. Karen will become more depressed and housebound. (Psychiatrist)

A phobic anxiety state (Sally 9.11) must not languish too long. (Psychiatrist)

In the long term 'disordered' children would:

> Continue to find gratification for their dependent needs in terms of psychiatric patient identity, perhaps for life.
>
> Hersov, 1960, p.144

This theory supported particularly powerful prognostications (NHS/HAS, 1995, Section 343):

> *As I see it, the only alternative (for Judy's) anxiety state, with hysterical and manipulative overlay, will be a long chronic neurotic life. (Psychiatrist)*

The case for preventing children like Judy becoming 'housebound', and April (subsequent subsection), a 'neurotic adult', was robustly argued, but the empirical evidence was mixed, and sometimes thin. For example, few long-term studies support the proposition that non-school attendance was deleterious. The idea originated in the work of Tyrer and Tyrer (1974) who concluded that one in three children who refused school or truanted were at risk of neurotic illness in adulthood:

> School refusal in girls should be viewed with greater foreboding than in boys, as they are more likely to develop neurosis in adult life ... School refusal in boys may be thought of as a temporary disturbance occurring at a vulnerable stage of development, particularly if it occurs before the age of eleven, whereas in girls it is more likely to be the first manifestation of a constitutional tendency towards neurotic maladjustment.
>
> Ibid., p.419

In contrast, Baker and Wills (1978) found little evidence that prolonged periods of absence from school was harmful. Valles and Oddy (1984) argued that resolving family conflict was more important than getting the youngster back to school: 'Whether the child returned to school or not made little difference to later adjustment at work.'

Berg (1981) concluded that:

> School refusal affects boys and girls equally ... There are indications of a relationship with affective or neurotic disorders in adult life. Severe truancy in primary school and in the first few years of secondary school appears to have implications in adult life. This has so far only been established in boys.
>
> Ibid., p.208, – Emphasis Added

Subsequently, Berg (1982) reported a longitudinal outcome study of one hundred school refusing adolescents. He identified a high incidence of persistent emotional and social difficulties in thirty-three per cent, three years after treatment, and twenty per cent after ten years. By 1987 his stance was solid: 'school phobia' could be a precursor to major psychiatric problems in adulthood, referencing this to the paper by Tyrer and Tyrer (1974).

So, the evidence for just one theoretical claim about the long-term implications for a child who has little education remained unclear. If two thirds of children were unaffected, then there would be efficiency gains in identifying the group requiring specialist resources. This is an example of why practice should be evidence based.

Overwhelming Rivals

Several tactics were employed when there was a high level of rivalry for case control. One was to give a poor prognosis. April (12.10) was in danger of mental illness because her foster mother was going blind, her elderly foster father was an invalid, and her adoptive brother was 'crippled by neurotic problems'.

> *April lacks the intellectual capacity for adapting to these very difficult circumstances ... obvious that she has very good attachment ... but because of the parents' illnesses and personal problems, it is a household in which it is difficult to grow up. Therefore, it is essential to separate her from her family for at least part of the time,*

otherwise she will develop into the same housebound-dependent individual that her brother is. (Psychiatrist)

Another tactic was to link behaviour and emotional states to the 'unconscious' mind. Ann (12.11) had:

Been stealing for four years. Until then she never questioned that she only saw her father four times a year, but another girl in a similar position raised it in her mind. Stealing dates from then and became progressively worse since puberty two years ago. (Psychiatrist)

A third strategy to ward off rivals and one which could be very valuable to other agencies, is the provision of a new perspective:

It is noteworthy that Ann is conscious that she steals because she is angry and, that when her stealing arouses her mother's anger, she steals all the more. I dare say that the pressure of puberty and the fact that she has a boyfriend, has not made her difficulty any less, but rather more. (Psychiatrist)

Agents who can offer such different perspectives into casework should be seeded in child welfare agencies to allow these ways of thinking to be available for more children.

Finally perhaps the provision of a solution is the most powerful tactic of all:

Stealing from mother and stepfather … They have no other complaints. The stealing has caused considerable tension in the home. Mother would not like the idea of separation from daughter, especially if it involved the girl returning to her father … Mother told me, if it helped, she would most readily agree to a period of separation. (Psychiatrist)

Attitudes to Women and Girls

We should look upon the female state as being, as it were, a deformity, though one which occurs in the natural course of nature.

Aristotle

Because a key objective of this book is to describe the nature of troubled and troublesome girls as seen through the eyes of CAMHSs, the remainder of this chapter offers thorough exposure to the original text. It was redolent with views concerning women as mothers, girls growing into women (Cain, 1991), and their relationships. It reflected the social values of the early decades of the twentieth century when mothers had a duty to care for children (Davin, 1978) with patience and self-sacrifice, and act as the 'emotional housekeepers', and the 'natural custodians of childhood' (Eleanor Rathbone).

> *One can clearly identify (Jenny's 15.10) mother as the problem, she gives her husband absolutely no support. (Psychiatrist)*

From the 1920s, the doctors in child health clinics imparted the skills of mother craft to inadequate women. Child guidance clinics developed in the 1930s to assist with 'maladjusted' children, who, because of poor mothering, were not benefiting from education. In this clinic of the late 1970s, the cult of motherhood, reinforced by psychodynamic theory, remained strikingly vibrant (Figes, 1978), and unmodified by feminist perspectives (Harding, 1987).

Lindsay's mother had 'no family and received an institutional childhood' therefore her parenting skills would be poor (Adcock and White, 1985). In the case of Lucy:

> *Given her own difficult life (mother) has strong feelings of guilt, which all too easily dominate her life. Her guilt about failing as a mother is easily elicited by Lucy, who often uses verbal statements to challenge her mother's love for her. This has led to a very stressful relationship between Lucy and her mother that continues to be psychologically damaging to both of them. (General Practitioner)*

Clare's mother had a:

> *Complex adoption background. She started her search (for her mother). She feels rejected by her own mother and her adopted*

43

mother died when she was thirteen. After the birth of her daughter, she had intense postnatal depression and stayed in hospital for eight months. She loves her daughter but is inconsistent because of her anger and frustration about her own mother. (Psychiatrist)

Inadequate mothers and invisible fathers were a striking feature.

A Blame Culture

The assessor's search for influential people in children's lives began and ended with mothers. As a result, they felt completely responsible for the situation (Nicholson and Ussher, 1992):

Sometimes (mother) is loving and caring, at others she becomes the child and Clare the parent ... obviously a long-standing pattern by the ease with which each slips into their role reversal. (Over several months of interviews) mother gradually developed a more positive attitude to herself. However her swings from rational to irrational in her role as mother were repeated as wife, sometimes subjugate slave, at others a director. (Psychiatrist)

Alex's (10.2) mother 'seemed to have a capacity for creating delinquency in her children' (Psychiatrist). Michelle (14.1) and her mother were seen for five months until mother refused to attend family meetings:

'There is no point. I don't like (the psychiatrist's) methods which heap pain upon me (and provoke feelings of) misery and insecurity.'

Later, Michelle's mother asked for a 'break from her confused and difficult daughter' whom she 'resented for involving the professionals'. A psychiatric social worker identified conflicts and difficulties but saw Jean's mother as weak and blameworthy:

Mother depressed throughout the menopause. Chose to have a sixth child at forty, but now feels that it was unfair on the child because it is as if she was an only child. Mother has been depressed since the family left the farm twenty-two years ago and has put on weight.

Jean's complete withdrawal and suicidal remarks have frightened Mother. Mother has played a large part in Jean's problems.

Most women were very self-critical. Rita's mother said that her daughter's overdose occurred because since the birth of a fifth child who had a disability, she had 'neglected' the children. Fixation on the performance of the mother meant that the distress in the family that led to Rita's mother, brother, and sister taking overdoses of drugs was ignored.

Parental Control

Lucy's mother had 'no longer got control over Lucy because she cannot make her return to school'. Parental shortfalls were instantly connected to the mother's childhood experiences. Of Alex's mother, it was said:

Treatment here is going to be fairly difficult. Ideally, intensive casework is needed with mother to find out what happened in her childhood to lead her to be a mother who is unable to be warm and controlling. (Psychiatrist)

A simple instruction was issued:

I have advised her to go out of her way to give Alex extra attention and care and control. (Psychiatrist)

A mother who was unable to be controlling by virtue of her own rearing, was commanded to provide control and achieve the previously impossible. This invective supported by 'intensive casework' to provide her with 'insight' into her failure, was a startling exposition of an oppressive approach (see Chapter VI). There was evidence that this 'immature little waif' was being sexually abused by her stepfather (a theme discussed in detail in Chapter V). However, her mother was construed as neglectful because she allowed Alex to 'wander the streets and have boyfriends'. This conflicted with Alex's mother 'not (being) keen for her to go to the hostel' and agreeing to admission only on condition that Alex could 'try a term and come home if she dislikes it'. Alex only stayed at the hostel for four months and then went home at her mother's request. If, indeed, Alex was being abused, the system had failed her, and her mother. Equally, it was evident that her mother wanted to care for her.

Emotional Distance

Emotional proximity to significant people was measured and connected to separation experiences. At the extremes some mothers were 'overinvolved' and 'overprotective', at a mid point they were 'ambivalent', and at the other extreme 'rejecting'. Sally's (9.11):

> *School phobia is partly related to the very overprotective attitude of mother, and the strong bonding between mother and daughter. (Psychiatrist)*

Being 'Mummy's girl' was 'unhealthy', even for pre-pubescent children:

> *Compliant and good and her mother is her sole companion. Her stomach pains are a manifestation of separation anxiety. Mother clings to daughter even more than daughter does to mother. (Psychiatrist)*

'Overprotection' produced 'an immature girl with an egocentric view of the world'. Jasmine (14.10) was a:

> *Pleasant girl, who related extremely badly to her parents. Mother has given up on her ... stepfather sees her as embarrassing ... A tremendous emotional gulf exists between mother and daughter. (Psychiatrist)*

Girls had to be liberated from carers who were trapping them in childhood, and the residential placements achieved this. When Lindsay (14.10) entered the hostel she was 'moving away from mother and her mother is depressed about it'. In general, the clinic saw residential placement as an act of rescue. Gill's (11.2):

Mother has a rather immature personality herself, and has been unable to make a satisfying relationship with this girl. The girl is very disturbed. Her main problem being separation anxiety as a result of extreme overt rejection by mother who has resented her from birth. (General Practitioner)

The psychiatric social work record (written six months previously) offered some possibilities for work with the family:

Mother admits that she completely rejected the baby at birth and never formed a close bond, but she wants to try and get along.

This is a good example of how opportunities to work on change whilst the child stayed at home were overlooked. Mary's (13.6) mother was a single parent with three children:

Reared strictly (the last of five children) and does not trust her mother … Mother finds difficulty in relating to her children at any stage of their development. She reacts harshly to the children stealing yet cannot influence or change their behaviour. I suspect she must be an insecure person who when cornered or severely threatened, cannot put the children's needs first. Stealing was a threat and she responded by throwing them out (into care for six weeks). (General Practitioner)

In contrast, a head teacher said mother was 'caring and in opposition to the education system in the area'. This was confirmed six months later when the educational psychologist assessed Mary and found that she had a significant relationship with her mother:

IQ. 114, Verbal 96, Performance 1.32 … Therefore full IQ is of limited usefulness. Some authors suggest a relationship between inadequate or inappropriate parent-child interaction and a test profile of this nature. Mary sees her mother in a positive way.

Six months later Mary's mother was reluctant to see the psychiatrist regularly:

'We thought it a school and not a psychiatric clinic. I feel that the last thing (Mary) needs at present is to feel rejected by me, which I know she would feel (if we came to the clinic).'

Psychotherapeutic support could not overcome high levels of rejectiveness and expressed emotion. This drove more invasive intervention and one that the model of decision making (Chapter IX) addresses. Deb (9.3) was 'overprotected (and) rejected' arising from her mother's 'ambivalent' feelings towards her. Deb had some physical disabilities, and her mother declared her 'abnormal, a monster' and requested hospital or residential care. The Psychiatric Social Worker noted:

A very disturbed mother-daughter relationship rooted in mother feeling that the child is physically and emotionally damaged … Mother denies the obvious rejection. Mother has been ambivalent since the birth of the child, and has overprotected, her Mother has underlying depression, poor self-esteem and marital problems. (Psychiatric Social Worker)

For two years Deb's mother received psychiatric social work support, but the 'relationships at home' continued to be 'tense and hostile'. There were fears that mother would 'abuse her'. The Psychiatrist concluded:

Mother cannot modify her attitude, the youngest boy is her favourite.

Deb spent thirty-two months away from 'from mother's domination' in the hostel. Taking two years to decide that 'modifications' had not occurred, failed to take the child's timescales into account. If the assessor were balancing the needs of parent and child then such decisions would benefit from discussion by all parties (Bryer, 1988).

Female Children

In contrast with society's preoccupation with the sexuality of girls (McRobbie, 1978) the predominantly male CAMHT staff seemed to regard it as mysterious and best ignored. This was a factor in the infantilisation of adolescent girls. So, assessors did not relate Jean's (12.8) non-attendance at school for two months to concerns about being 'overweight and very self-conscious', or to early puberty 'Menses at ten', but to 'phobias'.

Richardson's study of girls in approved schools found that women who were in positions to define girls as delinquent, showed no reluctance to do so, but men did.

> There is a seam of something we might vaguely call chivalry runs through our society, and while women in the main are more realistic about their own sex, most men were afraid of their mixed guilt and anger at the worst demonstrations of women and girls. Going wrong.
>
> Richardson, 1969, p.23

Girls in the empirical world were rarely described as delinquent. This was not, however, to protect them, as Richardson argued, but a strategy to justify mental health services. Delinquent girls were the business of other agencies. It follows that the label 'delinquent' ensured that the approved school had some clients.

Regulating Women and Girls

Assessors held a strong hand of cards to justify their interventions. High cards, about the essential features of satisfactory mothering, a joker, about girls who were out of control, and a trump card, which defined either the child or the mother as 'mentally ill'. High levels of expressed emotion between mother and daughter were regarded as unhealthy:

> *I am sure that Lucy does have some anxieties about school and is rather sensitive to teasing e.g. about her teeth. When she was originally ill, her anxieties about school escalated and she became reluctant to return. However, this has now developed into a power struggle between Lucy and her mother, with Lucy proving to her mother that she no longer has got control over Lucy. (Psychiatrist)*

The hostel was a useful device for separating the quarrelling parties. Jasmine (14.6) was in a 'battling relationship with her mother'. Hollie's (14.9) mother 'has no control. Hollie provokes her and enjoys exerting power … two people at war with themselves and each other'. There was seemingly no way, other than separation, of modifying these unseemly women who:

> Scrap and fight over little things. Daughter tells mother she is a 'rotten stinking git', she 'can't stand it at home' and wants to go away. Mother suggests that she goes into care. (Psychiatrist)

Nina's mother:

> Found it difficult to maintain control. With all these worries mother turned to Nina for support. I have seen them quarrelling and shouting at each other like two unhappy children. Mother says, 'All Nina does is make me suffer.' (Psychiatrist)

The powerful assessors took charge:

> She would benefit from going away from the many anxieties created by her mother. (Psychiatrist)

And disciplined wayward and assertive girls (Chapter VII):

> In my opinion, Lucy (14.4) has developed an ability to manipulate close relationships in a way that is damaging to both parties concerned. Her behaviour is motivated by the mistaken belief that this establishes her role and her importance in the relationship. I do not see much likelihood that Lucy will change this belief or her behaviour as long as she and her mother are both living together. (Psychiatrist)

Complete responsibility for family distress was vested with many children:

> I consider that Lucy needs a period of time away from home so that she can be helped to alter her perceptions of her family, and can experience an alternative set of relationships where she will not find it so easy to generate guilt. (Psychiatrist)

Any further protestations were often overpowered by reference to long-term harm, 'she (Connie 15.2) could be an awkward and explosive adult.' (Psychiatrist)

Women, Girls, and Madness

Women are the majority users of mental health services. Historically the view has abounded that they are mentally fragile, readily neurotic (Miles, 1989; Showalter, 1987), irrational and devious.

> *Mother is deliberately keeping (Sally) home (from school) for no apparent reason. (Psychiatrist)*

Their hysterical, inferior, and spiritually evil nature was connected to their biology (Brumberg, 1982).

Mothers were frequently diagnosed as having poor mental health. The mothers of Amy, Frances, and Ruth were 'respectively': 'chronic anxiety state', weak, depressed and strung up, highly anxious and Margaret's, 'family depends on mother's moods. She is labile and very neurotic'. Such descriptions underpinned major interventions:

> *Mother's abnormal and unusual attitude to Margaret swings from gross hostility and rejection with occasional punishment, to gross overconcern and panic coupled with retribution and blame. Today mother is very agitated, querying everything, adopting a self-deprecatory attitude, pessimistic and anxious about the smallest details.*

> *Mother is not fit to care for Margaret and needs psychiatric treatment. Margaret will be exposed to very agitating talk and behaviour from mother, which will affect her stability and schooling. (Psychiatrist)*

These women were not considered rational:

> *Mother's gross anxiety may lead her to turn it (the hostel) down because she fears she will be seen as a bad mother or some other self-deprecatory idea. (Psychiatrist)*

Incompetent, disruptive adults were avoided by giving asylum to the child:

For the good of the whole family, Margaret needs to go to the hostel. This will give mother a rest and treatment, relieve some sources of anxiety, and give Margaret stable care by responsible adults. (Psychiatrist)

Margaret's mother was portrayed very differently in a subsequent psychiatric social work account of 'a home visit'. She said she was 'torn apart ... assailed by doubts' about Margaret being admitted to the hostel. These doubts were reinforced by her husband's parents who felt that it was ill-advised. Margaret's mother had taken an overdose, ostensibly because her husband had said that he:

Could not take any more of Margaret, he is so angry he is going to drive his car into a brick wall. (In discussion father said) 'Margaret is upsetting my wife,' I don't want to know this. 'I'm getting rid of her' (to the hostel); Mother felt her whole world crumbling. 'He's a lovely man. I can't have him destroyed.' She spoke of her physical abuse of Margaret over the past year and how sometimes her husband had to separate them. The violent episodes seem to intensify her doubts about the hostel. 'Is this a conspiracy by the agencies to take my daughter away?' (Psychiatric Social Worker)

Mothers were largely ignored and attention focussed on the child. Girls had 'a constitutional tendency to neurotic maladjust-ment' (Tyrer and Tyrer, 1974, p.419):

No evidence of anything other than a fairly severe anxiety state with considerable hysterical and manipulative overlay (Karen 12.0). (Psychiatrist)

Jo (12.8) was:

Of an age where an increase in emotional instability very commonly occurs. Jo is morose and aggressive when asked to go to school. (Psychiatrist)

A wide band of children were held to need psychiatric care, from those who were 'obstinate, oversensitive, and (had) a general anxiety about life' (Gail 11.8), to those like Susan (15.0) who felt:

Very different, that everyone looks at her, thinks her odd, based on their knowledge that her mother is mentally ill and she lives in a strange family. She seems to be one of those who have grown-up in a situation where the family standard of what is normal and sane has been incompatible with the standard of outside society, and the patient herself has thought 'someone is mad but who is it? Is it me? Is it my mother? Or is it the world of reality?' (Psychiatrist)

Audit of the types of children who are being defined as having mental health problems (one in five in 1999) is essential. The thresholds seem very low.

Cure was a protracted business because:

She has strains from many sides, the adjustment to ordinary household life at the hostel, to social life at school; and the intellectual demands at school, and the separation anxiety of a girl who has never formerly left her parents, but 'nevertheless' has many times felt herself to be in acute danger in her own home. (Psychiatrist)

Easing children's minds appears to have been very difficult work because Susan's fear of madness remained for a long time.

Most of this commentary is critical of professional performance. Using the audit as a basis for dialogue could produce some modifications with ease.

The Marginalisation of Men

The association of mental disturbance with mothering was so strong that men were largely ignored. Jo's (12.8):

Psychopathology is reasonably straightforward. (She has) depression superimposed on a personality that all her life has been emotionally insecure. (Psychiatrist)

Jo's (12.8) mother was 'depressed and menopausal, a part-time infant helper' and apparently unable to give the care and attention her daughter needed. However, there was quite a lot of evidence to suggest that Jo was a victim of sexual abuse (Chapter VIII) and not her mother's lack of care:

> *Jo is sobbing, depressed and reluctant to go to school. She frequently goes to the WC at night. Urine tested NAD. Temper tantrums since eighteen months of age. Jo has always expected her sister (one year older) to protect her, and she has until recently. Father is a solicitor. Very tolerant but increasingly exasperated with Jo to such an extent that he has been vomiting before he leaves for work with the struggle to get her out of bed and in the car for school. (Psychiatrist)*

Little interest was shown in Jo's father, and a long account ended:

> *Summary. For no reason apparent in the history, Jo has developed from a selfish and demanding person before the deaths of her grandparents (four months previously) into a surly, hateful, depressed girl. Nothing to account for her obvious feeling of insecurity. (Psychiatrist)*

Inevitably, Jo's mother suggested that it must be her 'mistakes' that caused the problems. This illustration of how the value base influences performance is explored further (in the next chapter) in considering the formulations that the agency produced. In the main, men were either benign or uninteresting, or they were 'sissy' or 'mad':

> *I recommend that (Sandra 11.6) is admitted (to the hostel). Home is extremely disturbed and she needs a period of safety and security. The source of stress at home is father. I am entirely dependent on mother's account, but he may have serious and dangerous psychiatric disorder. (Psychiatrist)*

Because men were largely invisible, this drew attention to the few who were very intrusive, and it will be suggested in Chapter VII that they had malign intentions.

Summary

The following extracts from the case record about Kim (11.10) draw out the aspects of the ideology that had a major impact on the services given namely:

1. The hysterical/neurotic nature of females.
2. The ready recourse to mental or physical disorder, and exclusion of other matters of significance.
3. The high level of interest in the problematical characteristics and behaviours of mothers.
4. The oppression of mother and child.
5. The disinterest in other family members.

A second stepfather had recently joined Kim's family of three older stepsisters and twins three years younger. Kim's doctor wrote:

> *She comes from a very disturbed family background in which previous daughters have had similar problems during early teens and mother is not the best at managing. However, I feel that Kim is potentially the worst of them all.*

After referral, Kim and her mother were seen by an Educational Psychologist who found mother:

> *Extremely agitated and depressed and continually shouting abuse at Kim. She said that she was totally unmanageable and she was deprived of affection and wants to see her own father and godfather. She is very jealous of the twins and of the older sisters who have 'abandoned' her.*

Kim's mother told the Psychiatric Social Worker that she feared Kim would:

> *Damage her brain with this behaviour (uncontrollable screaming). Family relationships seem to be very stormy most of the time and come to a head in adolescence. (One of the older girls) has reported mother to the police as cruel. The three older girls are of the same*

father and mother blames him for all the wrongs. I feel that mother is very rejecting of them, linked with her feelings to father.

The psychiatrist concluded that Kim was:

Really very disturbed indeed. The parents find it extraordinarily difficult to contain her behaviour which is immature, omnipotent and eccentric. I gather she is helped by Diazepam, and the parents feel she would be totally uncontrollable if she was not having it. The parents' description suggests it is unlikely we will solve the problem as an outpatient and she may need admission but I will delay that for the time being.

High levels of family conflict are present but the primary interests of the agency dominate the direction pursued:

The history is striking. She has had a chaotic childhood but appears to have been relatively well adjusted until six months ago when she began to develop violent infantile temper tantrums. If her mother is to be believed, she was not subject to them before. The possibility of early psychosis cannot be excluded, but in view of the sudden change, I think we ought to exclude any progressive intracranial lesion. (Psychiatrist)

Mother was 'unreliable excited and upset', and said she 'felt that everyone was blaming me'. Kim (12.5) was admitted to the Adolescent Inpatient Unit:

As an emergency following a severe breakdown in family relationships. Kim felt that she could do what she liked in relationship with mother and, when frustrated, reacted violently. Mother's response was histrionic and she appeared unable to cope with Kim. The situation was aggravated by interference by an older sister … (Psychiatrist)

The women had to be brought under control:

Our main task in the early stages of treatment was to establish in

> *Kim's mind that she was not in a position to control her family and she had to accept normal adult controls. Kim's behaviour seemed at times bizarre and lacking in normal social validation. We have, therefore, suspected the possibility of psychotic illness. We concluded it was a manifestation of infantile personality development as a result of eccentric child rearing. We noticed that mother was also rather eccentric and infantile in her behaviour responses to stress, for example, excessive tempers, if she could not have her own way and walking out of situations which she could not face. (Psychiatrist)*

There could be many explanations. Others less interested in mothers or developmental immaturity, might have pursued the information that Kim was:

> *Near to puberty … likes her stepfather to tuck her in and kiss her goodnight. Mother has given up being a nursing assistant because of Kim … Interference by her older sister has led to a relapse. (Psychiatrist)*

It is impossible to do more than suggest that the arrival of stepfather and the high levels of family conflict may be related. The point here is that it is possible simply from reading the records for an evaluator to draw the worker's attention to the possibility of other perspectives.

Conclusion

At this point, the structure of the organisation and its relationship with the outside world has been depicted. This was an agency that worked hard at definition not only of the inside and outside of children but of itself, and particularly its boundaries. The combination of a common set of beliefs, 'many joinings between models' (Freehill, 1973), and an etiquette determined by a hierarchical set of social relations produced, enormous power. The issues of distress, control and socialisation accompanying the children were enclosed in that patriarchal architecture which concentrated on mothering. These factors transposed and hid the regulatory function of the agency and, therefore, its similarity to

Social Services. Some intriguing practices are emerging, for instance, the child's apparent fear of separation from her family became a real experience because they were moved into residential care. Finally, typical narratives about girl children have been presented. This exploration of the ideology has offered a basis from which to explore the daily work.

Chapter IV
NEW TEXT

I think it is likely that Penny is uncertain about her relationship with her mother, and that she used her non-school attendance as a powerful means of establishing a central role in the family. The consequence of Penny staying home is that (mother) has constantly had Penny as the focus of her attention, and inadvertently has given Penny control of the situation through the use of a type of emotional blackmail. In my opinion, Penny has developed an ability to manipulate close relationships in a way that is damaging to both parties. (Psychiatrist)

Extracts from a representative case (Angela 13.7) show the general pattern of practice (Kazdin, 1981) from referral to case closure (Sheldon, 1983). The process is then examined to see what was gained and what avoided by this way of working. Even during the early encounters between users and providers, assessment and treatment are closely entwined. This may be one reason why the separation of purchaser and provider within an agency, or between agencies, is difficult to achieve.

Reception

I am sure it is an anxiety state. Started school this term but not managed a full day (in three weeks). The family recently moved (from another county). Angela was beginning to have difficulties before she moved. She is very upset at leaving her grandparent's. (General Practitioner)

First Interview

Patient refuses to get out of car or go to school. Okay until (six months ago) had German measles then a cold, then became reluctant to return to school. Mother pushed her; she spent time in sickbay. (Mother) got breast lump. This upset Angela who ran to her maternal grandparents. Mother had postnatal depression. Maternal grandmother helped. Breastfed – thrived. Paternal grandfather died three years ago. Separations to stay with grandparents. Mother feels there is a need for her to break away. Menses six months ago. Never excelled at school. Went to local comprehensive for two days but needed lot of help from father. Mother managed to walk her there but she was too upset. Father – maintenance engineer, forty-five. Duodenal ulcer worse under stress. Father feels he is overprotective. Mother forty. Father says midwives insisted wife breastfeeds and made her feel a failure. Mother says she nags about school work as she herself was by her father. Her father was clever, she wasn't, but could have made more of herself. Sees daughter as clever. (Psychiatrist)

An Assessment of Need

Positive aetiological factors: only child. Mother – neurotic depression. Dependence on maternal grandparents. Typical school phobia needs urgent action to stop chronicity … Hope parents now see that they must be much firmer for her sake. (Psychiatrist)

A Care Plan

Try Meprobamate to boost her confidence. Parents and school must be firm in getting her there and not letting her use the sickbay. (School) staff must understand that her symptoms are the result of normal anxiety and do not stem from any physical cause. (Psychiatrist)

Admission to the Adolescent Psychiatric Unit

(One month on) A crisis arose. She was admitted. Angela settled well and she will try to be back at school with help from our staff. When we have accomplished this, we shall only be touching on the surface of the problem. Both parents are showing many signs of considerable stress, and family work will be essential to stop the whole family disrupting. (Psychiatrist)

Assessment

Striking contrast after initial homesickness. She is confident, calm and enjoys herself. Father negatively surprised says, 'You didn't get her shopping did you? You'll never get her to school. If only she could be happy, we could be happy'. Mother says: 'You're killing your father.' What precipitated father into admitting her? (Psychiatrist)

Child's View

'I don't want to go home. I will only be all right when they have sorted themselves out.' (Psychiatric record)

Residential Placement

Four months later there was an:

Emergency hostel admission. Angela was manipulating everyone, announcing she was going back to school and then not. Parents became increasingly tense and distraught, and it came to the point where she was refusing to accept any control. Angela has attended school regularly since her admission (to the adolescent unit), so our object in admitting her was successful. (Psychiatrist)

Letter to Education Officer

Should do well in school if she has academic stability. Her problems were partly precipitated by the move from the west. (Psychiatrist)

(The average age of admission to the hostel was fourteen years and two months.)

Letter to Referrer

No medication. Prognosis guarded. Thin, pale girl, histrionic behaviour initially, no psychotic features. Manipulative at the clinic, school, and with parents, however, she proved a capable girl who can cope with crowded places and communicate in large groups. She was discharged to the hostel when her refusal to accept help and control was greatly upsetting to her parents. (Psychiatrist)

A 'Social History'

Several attempts to return to school whilst in adolescent unit. Despite her parents' agreement to this management, father emphasised that the plan would not work and she would not attend school. (Psychiatrist)

New Care Plan

Now that she is at the hostel, we can begin to work with the family with a view to improving the overall stability.

Angela does not present any behavioural difficulties and should be conforming and sensible. She does not require any special treatment or care in school. (Psychiatrist)

Early Outcome

She has settled well at the hostel, and is attending school daily. Family interviews occurred at the clinic, and the Psychiatric Social Worker made regular home visits. (Psychiatrist)

Longer-term Outcome

She has changed very positively: a happy cheerful girl. She gives the impression she wants to work her way home. (Psychiatrist)

Unplanned Return Home

Angela stayed at the hostel for eighteen months (the median length of stay). Young people were expected to remain until completion of their secondary education. At her parents' request, Angela went home prematurely (aged 15.1). (Unplanned discharges occurred in seventeen per cent of cases.) Subsequently Angela's mother said:

Angela only went to the (CAMHT) because they were 'new to the district and didn't know where to turn'. Feels the 'stigma' and doesn't want to see the need for further help. (Psychiatrist)

Follow-up

The Psychiatric Social Worker tried, unsuccessfully, to re-establish family meetings with the psychiatrist because Angela was:

Refusing parental control, has punk boyfriend on fringes of drugs and delinquency, going to local den of iniquity. Father feels hurt and upset that she tells him to get out. Parents do not agree. Father feels pushed to limit – gave her a good hiding. No problems over school attendance. (Psychiatric Social Worker)

Angela's mother described:

Several hysterical incidents e.g. mother left her wedding ring on the table, father packed his case, daughter pushed mother over in an argument about the phone, ran out screaming when told could not go to all-night party, father brought her home and she locked herself in bedroom screaming. Parents' attitude: 'what have we done to deserve this? Why shouldn't we have some peace?' Don't exert authority in face of her hysterical temper. Mother says daughter has pubic lice and may have VD, strongly denied by daughter who admits to messing about but not sexual intercourse. Says: 'Why don't you both go and leave me?' I shall leave home as soon as I'm sixteen. (Psychiatric Social Worker)

Involving Other Agencies

Alternatives – clinic appointment but Angela would not come. (psychiatric) social work surprise visit home. Social Services if really beyond control, mother fears she would be put away with worse girls. Mother asks could she go back to hostel – I say need to come in to see Psychiatrist to discuss, but I doubt there is a vacancy. (Psychiatric Social Worker)

Retrospective Assessment

Not an Angela problem but a family problem. (Psychiatrist)
Willing to see whole family or parents. (Psychiatric Social Worker)

Case Closure

Father declined an interview, because he was having 'chest pains'.
His wife was seen by the Psychiatric Social Worker:

Now quite hostile and rejecting: 'If she won't do what we say,' 'she must get on with it and take the consequences. We can't be worried any more.' (Mother) will not accept that there is an underlying problem. The den has been raided by the police, daughter in a panic about photos taken there of her naked. Mother still believes that daughter has 'not had sexual intercourse'. Quite angry with friend's parents who have said Angela is a bad influence. Mother tried to blame everyone else. (Psychiatrist)

There was no further contact with the family.

It's a Kind of Magic

Angela has illustrated the process and content of service delivery. 'Assessment' and 'treatment' was delivered through, 'diagnostic (or) assessment interviews, family work, family group, family therapy, child psychotherapy, history (taking)' or 'small group' (for children only).

People received sustained attention often over long periods of time. For example Sally had appointments for twelve months, and after a gap of a few months, she was referred again (aged 12.10), and 'seen' for another eight months before being admitted to the hostel. Throughout this time, the psychiatric social worker regularly visited her parents(s) at home. Consistent support in this example for a total of fifty-eight months was greatly valued by the recipients.

'Seeing' and Talking

Various combinations of carers and children attended the initial interview with the Psychiatrist and Social Worker. Subsequently, the child was seen alone by the psychiatrist and the parent(s) by the Social Worker. Sometimes the child saw the Educational Psychologist for 'tests'. It was rare for a Child Psychotherapist to become involved.

'Appointment talk' used 'history taking', problem identification, observations of child behaviour and of the parent – child relationship 'to help with the management of her more difficult behaviour' and give the child's mother:

> *Insights into her relationship with Sally (and see that her) symptoms have an emotional basis. (Psychiatrist)*

'Talk' was directed at converting the family to the viewpoint of the assessors. Sue's (11.3):

> *Mother does not have a great deal of faith in the future bringing any improvement in her relationship with her daughter or in Sue settling into (new school). However, she is prepared to bring Sue to the clinic to see me, and I, therefore arranged another appointment. Sue did come to the appointment with me, and, in fact, agreed to come and see me again. (Psychiatrist)*

There seemed to be some 'guesswork':

> *Lindsay's (14.10) relationships and crush on lorry driver – whilst perhaps nothing bar banter and horseplay, may have provided the immediate trigger for her overdose ... The spark to ignite a considerable family pathology. (Psychiatrist)*

Even frank perplexity about the origins of decisions:

> *There is little doubt that father, who makes sexual advances and exposes himself to the girls, has had an adverse effect on all three girls' emotional development and adolescent adjustment. It must be this that led me to admit one to the adolescent unit and the other to the hostel for the maladjusted and to provide intensive support over a long period to all three girls. (Psychiatrist)*

There were similarities to the work of a 'medicine of tissues' (Foucault, 1977), in that symptoms could be described and treated, but the cause remained a mystery.

> *Having acute anxiety attacks, the cause is obscure, though it may be related to anxieties about growing up. She is developing increasing agoraphobia. I suggest that she is treated with Lorazepam. (Psychiatrist)*

Twenty-two days later, the Adolescent Inpatient Unit was struggling for clarification:

> *It is difficult to decide if it is separation anxiety or school phobia. Judy is very distressed at parting from the family. When they visit, both parents are anxious and ineffectual and allow her to control them in a maladaptive way. (Psychiatrist)*

Seven months after Judy returned home, she was again missing school:

> *There is no real evidence of anything other than a fairly severe anxiety state with considerable hysterical and manipulative overlay. (Psychiatrist)*

Judy had been 'assessed' for fifteen months and received talking and residential therapies. In an early interview she said: 'Nobody understands or cares.' This was prophetic and remained true, at least in part, for her, and most of the young people in this sample of children that were placed in residential care.

A Fusion of Processes

Assessment and treatment were not sequential, separate activities but were often fused in early 'therapeutic interventions'. These could occur at separate points within an interview, or in the same utterance:

If Kate not taking steps seriously (assessment) *and back to school by tomorrow, she would be admitted to the adolescent unit* (treatment). *(Psychiatrist)*

Change directed work was quickly under way. Kate had to stop being flippant. Given that the evidence gathering was so slim and largely based on the experience of being with the family, less highly trained workers could be used either from the outset, or after assessment to exclude mental illness. Entwining assessment and treatment served several functions:

- It gave additional justification for keeping the case.
- It obscured 'guesswork'.
- It overwhelmed dilemmas and discrepancies.

Currently, welfare organisations are splitting the task of assessing a person's needs from the provision of services. In order to service the organisational separation of 'purchase' and 'provision' to achieve this, it will be necessary to dissect the pre-existing practices to see how separate or entwined they are in the initial assessment work. Old practices die hard and, once provider services have been separated, the degree to which the providers are making fresh assessments and reconfiguring the new clients to match their resources, will need evaluation. Reducing the scope of any service requires giving up sovereignty and territory. Resistance may be high, and some agencies will give ground reluctantly.

A 'Medicine of Behaviour'

Early work with families produced 'new text' (Howe, 1994), a 'diagnosis' in a different language. The record that follows shows that this was achieved by processes of 'objectification', 'narrowing', and 'magnification', culminating in a 'solidified' construction. Father (thirty-one), stepmother (twenty-two), and Caroline (10.11) were (untypically) seen by the Child Psychiatrist in a paediatric clinic. Caroline had recently started to hide paper bags containing faeces in her bedroom. 'Father says she has "gone to pieces for about two years".'

The exploration of past events was cursory:

> *Last year she was fostered with a friend, but then the friend fell ill. Caroline went to stay with elderly friends of natural mother. After six months she was taking money. (Psychiatrist)*

The transposition of stealing to 'taking' which was a 'symptom of neurotic disturbance not conduct disorder' (Jasmine), justified the involvement of the CAMHT.

> *Eighteen months ago father remarried. They are angry because she hasn't fitted in. She lies. (Psychiatrist)*

Harsh parental attitudes and family discord, frequently encouraged 'rescue activity'. At this point Caroline was given a small voice:

> *She likes father and stepmother but thinks they do not like her. Doesn't know at all if dad likes her. Dad smacks her hand. (Psychiatrist)*

Caroline's profound statement, despite the presence of her carers, produced alternative living arrangements for Caroline:

> *Can't live with (?) she has too many children of her own. (Psychiatrist)*

The carers were not making a good impression:

> *Father and stepmother seem hypocritical and rejecting – obviously cannot be bothered, though they tried a little.*

By this juncture, Caroline was – not herself, not fitting in, a liar, unsure if she was loved, motherless and rejectable:

> *She does not know anything about her natural mother.*
> *Wishes: 'a horse'. (Psychiatrist)*

At this point, the reader is becoming convinced that the combination of the history and the attitude of the carers made the situation hopeless:

Caroline presents a very unhappy problem. The presentation of conduct disorder and encopresis is not surprising in view of the chaotic pillar to post existence she has led from birth. She desperately needs a caring secure home. Stepmother is trying very hard but is young and immature, and had difficulties in her own childhood. (Psychiatrist)

The pervasiveness of the medical model can be readily observed and construing children's behaviour as a manifestation of disease meant that 'conditions deteriorated' and 'complications developed'. Even if the model was a poor fit, it empowered practitioners. Chloe (14): 'took an overdose of paracetamol. Said she was upset because her boyfriend had ended their relationship. (Psychiatrist)' Chloe had 'personal counselling' for seven months. Despite this, her school attendance declined until 'she developed school phobia' (Psychiatrist).

Harriet (15.2):

Developed acute and severe school phobia. This became so severe that she developed hysterical blindness. (Psychiatrist)

Despite 'disease' sometimes developing before their eyes, and a familiarity with the family circumstances, this specialist agency appeared to be ineffective:

Chloe has been unable to verbalise any reasons for her school phobia. (Psychiatrist)

Another aspect of both medicine (Dowie and Elstein, 1988) and social work (Packman et al., 1986) is the milieu of emergency:

A crisis arose. Great family stress. Danger it will disrupt. (Psychiatrist)

These action-driven cultures use risk in the client's situation to catalyse alterations in the style of service delivery. As we see in this empirical data, this 'urgency' can also stem from:

> A single-minded model of the 'problem', its 'detection' and its 'solution' (which) helps to create the pressure under which child abuse professionals work.
>
> Stainton Rogers et al., 1989, p.50

The data shows that action was also driven by the need to solve the problem, to maintain the image of the agency, and sustain a belief in the efficacy of the remedies. Perhaps excitability in a system can be used as a signal for cautious performance appraisal.

Missing the Point

Interest in mental health is diverting and restricts the picture of the child's world. For example, worries about going to school were viewed as a 'projection' of psychological distress on to the world of school. Joy (12.7) moved school three times in three years. She was gradually becoming:

> *Very difficult, withdrawn and quiet. Long-term difficulties making friends – did not 'think anyone liked her'. (Educational Psychologist)*

A rich psychodynamic diet of 'strange mannerisms' and what Joy's father called her 'paranoia', were embellished by the 'history':

> *Kept in a separate nursery (after delivery), did not let go and walk independently until fourteen months. Mother supposed this showed lack of confidence. Between one and two years cried a lot. At eighteen months, mother was in hospital for ten days. She didn't want to go with mother when she returned to collect her. At just turned three she started at playgroup, went in screaming, but settled after mother left. At five she went through a period of excessive clinging to mother, even following her to the toilet. (Letter to Psychiatrist)*

Joy volunteered that her 'father didn't love her and had a quiet talk with her'. The focus on neuroses and developmental status meant that trying to help her settle at school or dangers at home did not come into the picture:

> *Health: No details obtained but she started her periods some months*

ago and they are established. She didn't want to know about them, didn't want to listen when mother tried to prepare her for them. Mother said at about ten years a film had been shown without any prior consultation with parents. It was very explicit and included intercourse. Mother feels that Joy is not ready for this and she started complaining of stomach pains after seeing it. (Psychiatrist)

Sometimes different reasons for the children's distress were suspected when the children were in the residential placements. After a year and a half at the hostel, Rhian (15.4) 'seems to be afraid of stepfather. Claims he made sex advances' (Hostel worker). Nine months later Rhian's younger sister told her: 'that father was responsible for her pregnancy.' He was later convicted of child sexual abuse. All along the assessors had been drawn to Rhian's 'anorexia'.

A six-week history of not keeping food down and not eating or drinking much and vomiting everything she does. Rhian has been depressed about and upset with her father because she was visiting her mother again. Last night mother's husband was verbally aggressive, though offering Rhian family life. Then she went to her father who was very angry that she was visiting her mother. Father disabled. Heavy drinker. (Psychiatrist)

Rhian and her siblings were made subject of Care Orders. Rhian's explanation for her distress was that 'Mum left home and my dad used to drink'. The assessors mimicked this:

Her present depression and physical symptoms developed at about the time that her father had to give up his council house, so that she was left with no home at all. (Psychiatrist)

Yet, even the record in the adolescent unit indicates that this was an unsatisfactory explanation:

Rhian has now been admitted to the (adolescent unit), and I hope we will be able to get to the bottom of her problem quickly. (Psychiatrist)

The text is suggesting that important material was often overlooked in these cases.

A 'Binary Construction'

> The reading of the type of case is conditional ... the definition and the remedy only hold until further notice.
>
> Giller and Morris, 1981, p.99

One of the most intriguing observations, and the one which provoked the ideas for the model of decision making (Chapter IX), was the shift from work with the child and family, to work just with the child. It was partly explained by the tensions arising from co-existing theories and competing models of practice discussed in Chapter III.

> *(Caroline) I will try conjoint family meetings in the hope that we can save something from the wreck. (Psychiatrist)*

However, these shifts were mainly driven by a two-dimensional formula which produced a choice of treatment modalities. Clinicians dabbled with a modern method of work with all the family but retained a fallback position of direct work with the child.

Initially, assessors allocated 'problems' to the child but coupled them with family problems. So creating a two-part 'diagnosis':

1. Conduct disorder: stealing ... Soiling, poor school progress (Caroline)
2. Unwanted. Mother neglected her. Father stresses all her negative qualities.

The child could be a problem individual or part of a problem family. In a similar way, social workers separated 'delinquent' children (Millham, 1978) from dysfunctional families (Giller and Morris, 1981). In addition to this useful ability to vacillate and recalibrate the style of work, any of the following could fracture the 'binary social construction':

- The ideology.
- Treatment failure.
- Routinised services and resources.

The residential remedies took care of the child but could not, for example, offer a whole family residency. So, where at first the origin of the child's behaviours was located in the malfunctions of the family group, this was diluted as work with the family faltered, and the retention of the case was in jeopardy. Despite sometimes sterling efforts to keep adults engaged in conversation, the worker terminated the struggle and produced a new equilibrium:

> *Father was angry and despairing. Twice he hit Caroline for stealing ... He asked if Caroline could be adopted ... I feel strongly that unless she is given a chance at the hostel, she will be increasingly at risk. (Psychiatrist after family meetings over nine months)*

The binary system had fragmented into two independent stars, and the 'family star' spun away into the ether. This was very evidently a 'child' and not a 'family-centred' universe. This answers part of the enigma. Assessors could justify either course of action by oscillating between family focussed and child focussed explanations for distress. This concurs with Giller and Morris's (1981) findings about social work that, factors 'which challenge the treatment model are reinterpreted, de-emphasised or recontextualised' (ibid., p.45) to meet the needs of the worker. This suggests that in any social world, social constructions can be evaluated in terms of the extent to which they act as:

- Failsafe mechanisms which encapsulate and resolve tensions and conflict in the discourse.
- Ways of preserving the agency.

The Interventions

This section considers the therapeutic services offered by the CAMHT, namely interviews, medication, and placements outside the family.

'TALK'

Caroline's 'long history of rejection from early infancy' was approached by 'conjoint family meetings'.

The only hope here is to try and work with the goodwill of her father and stepmother, to help them be more positive and overtly affectionate. At present they are reacting to all her negative behaviours. (Psychiatrist)

The voluntary contract (Chapter III) was dependent on the cooperation of carers and, therefore, very fragile. It was not possible to be honest about the inferences made by assessors:

I am afraid that however hard we work she may be abandoned by this couple. (Psychiatrist)

Even where the risk of significant harm was high, confidence was vested in the power of this technique:

I think she may already have been exposed to some quite severe punishment, and there is a danger in a situation like this of cruelty. (Psychiatrist)

Parents will often be highly resentful in being involved in both diagnosis and treatment plans, seeing themselves as sufferers and yet apparently being blamed. In the context often of parent/child hostility, the objective of the first interview may be limited to endeavouring to ensure that there will be a second. With the adolescent one must 'sell oneself' as being worth trusting and talking to.

Lumbsden-Walker, 1992, p.39

Interviews, particularly initial ones, were fraught and delicate:

At interview mother was manipulative, unwilling to compromise, did not impress me as the kind of mother who would work well with our staff. Clearly becomes prejudiced easily and sees things in extreme terms which can make her very difficult to work with. Mary (14.0) resembles mother in quickly becoming hostile if things don't go her way. (Psychiatrist)

The origins of this situation arose from the work that had been undertaken by referrers (Chapter II). Family doctors had problematised the child. To correct this, referrers must adopt practices which support family work. Initial attempts by clinic staff to do this were further undermined by the fragility of the 'voluntary' relationship with parents (Chapter III) as well as by their dominant interest in the child.

> *(Kirstie's) mother and stepfather have an unhappy relationship; mother encouraged Kirstie's neurotic behaviours to consolidate their relationship and to get at stepfather. (Psychiatrist)*

Whilst skills were well honed in, prescribing child-centred solutions for 'risky situations', the practitioners rarely shared their opinions with families:

> *My feeling is that this is not an educational problem but one of family relationships. Samantha is feeling very lonely and uncared for. (Psychiatrist)*

Retaining information was partly a power game, but it was also a way of tackling the high level of fragility surrounding the social relations between families and the clinic. A non-confrontative style avoided conflict. If families detected a whiff of criticism, they exercised their prerogative not to participate. Consequently, assessors went along with the already well honed, and now convenient, belief held by carers and others that there was something wrong with the child. Yet assessors recognised that the child was conflicted and terribly distressed by the behaviour and/or attitudes of adults (Peterson and Zill, 1986). Assessors chose not to voice this. It was 'better to be baddies' than provoke conflict and risk losing the case. As I shall argue later, the child paid the price of failure to continue family-based work.

Carers showed few signs of owning any part in the problem. Even the medical/confidential milieu could not erase this resistance. Other factors undermining a cooperative endeavour were the intimidating Dickensian atmosphere of the clinic, the stigma of association with psychiatry and for some the inconvenience of daytime appointments. The rules of engagement needed to be publicised. An agency confident in its helping strategies can contract with users in a way that will help all parties to stay together through the hard times. In this respect, the coercive powers held by statutory agencies have positive benefits in the initial stages. Failing to reframe the construction around the family was the single greatest performance shortfall. It produced a conspiracy between the adults which was sustained and obscured by:

- Ready access to rescue remedies.
- Denying parents the right to participate fully in major decisions.

(Vivien's mother was 'totally self-interested', Natasha's 'put her own needs (first) and is unavailable due to depression'. Sally's mother was 'very preoccupied with her broken marriage.')

- The culture of voluntarism and prescriptive behaviour which avoided difficult issues.
- Poor mediation skills.

The inability to be honest with families resulted in subversive protective actions. In Lindsay's case, where sexual abuse was acknowledged, a secret plan to protect her siblings, who were still in the home, was concocted by a psychiatrist, with a nurse in charge of their disabled fathers respite care:

> *It is extremely difficult to make a plan in a case like this. There is little doubt that father makes sexual advances and exposes himself to the girls. The problem continues for the two younger ones, so the plan should be for father to only come home for occasional weekends.*

Honesty was risky because:

1. The rule of confidentiality would be weakened;
2. Conflict would arise;
3. The child could be withdrawn from treatment by the parent;
4. The system's failure to cure the case might be exposed;
5. The case could be lost to Social Services.

Any of these factors could bring the competency of the CAMHT into question.

The empirical evidence of the consequences of non-confrontation lends support to intentions of the Children Act (1989) to form partnerships with families built on honesty and respect (Aldgate, 1991; DH, 1995 (a)). The theme of 'confrontation' is revisited in the exploration of the way children were 'reformed' (Chapter VI).

MEDICATION

The prescription of drugs to modify moods and behaviours was a defining aspect of the medicine of behaviour. Often medical referrers had tried a drug treatment. They and other referrers were often attracted by this 'additional' and unique, service available in the CAMHSs.

Assessors showed no reticence about using this technology. Connie (13.7) had 'periods of high elation and deep gloom'. She was prescribed 'Penothrazine' but 'the tablets made her feel "bad, a bit silly". No concentration. Looked a bit like an old dishcloth' (Psychiatrist). So the drug was substituted by 'Chlorpromazine'. Karen's (13.10) 'increasing agoraphobia (was) treated with Lorazepam' (Psychiatrist). Eight days later she was 'calmer but still unable to get to school'. Somewhat unconfidently the medication was altered:

> *Anafranil ... becoming increasingly depressed. I have said that if she is not getting to school in the next few days, she will have to be admitted. When this pressure is put on, she will find it very difficult to manage and will be better off in hospital. (Psychiatrist)*

Two days later Karen was admitted to the adolescent unit. After three months Karen was back home, but the:

> *Clinical picture has changed little – she is behaving in a domineering and aggressive way. Advised Diazepam (tranquilliser) to help her about going to school and an outpatient appointment. If there has been no progress in a few weeks time, then I think we should insist that she be readmitted. (Psychiatrist)*

The persistence with medication as the treatment of choice was remarkable and may suggest that poor outcomes were uncommon.

RESIDENTIAL CARE

The Adolescent Psychiatric Unit was not studied directly but it provided a variety of treatments: drugs, psychiatric nursing care, group therapy, family and individual talk, occupational therapy, and schooling on or off site (Steinberg, 1986; Wolkind and Gent, 1989). Betty (13.9) is an example of the children (fifty-two per cent) who were admitted there before moving on to the hostel. Her mother thought that she was 'a badly damaged mentally ill person'. The assessors thought that Betty had 'severe symptoms' of an 'acute psychotic breakdown and an unusual form of epilepsy' precipitated by:

> An overdose … peculiar attacks at school when her behaviour and speech were almost psychotic … not a simple reactive disorder, though exposed to a lot of stress as a result of two bereavements. (Psychiatrist)

The inpatient assessment concluded:

> In retrospect, her clinical appearance was a prolonged post-epileptic confusional state with superimposed hysterical features … Under stress, regressed to baby talk. (Psychiatrist)

Relapses of 'psychotic illness' could be produced by 'exposure to rather intense and not very helpful relationships' at home. When ready, the move to the hostel provided these children with ongoing, 'adequate psychiatric supervision and good support'.

Conclusion

This reading of the process and content of the service has shown that employing 'professionals' is an investment in the 'eyes of the beholders'. It has demonstrated that the medical/psychiatric gaze is sufficiently accessible through their records to allow some performance evaluation by a lay person.

My impression is that in this cohort of cases, the CAMHT

was set up to fail. Parents and others expected them to cure sick children. This thoroughly undermined any attempts to locate the source of problems in the child's environment. Agencies 'therefore' are interdependent, and one of the goals of interagency collaboration must be to adjust practices to maximise the effectiveness of each agency. This is very obvious but the objective may be lost in power struggles.

Working with children in distress is difficult and some glue is needed to help parties stay together in the hard times. In this respect, statutory agencies have a perhaps unappreciated advantage in being able to use coercion in the stages before partnership and cooperation develop. Rather than being derogatory about this, it should be regarded as an asset, as the child protection meeting process has demonstrated. Given (as will be said in Chapter VII) how disempowered children are, the powers and duties of the Children Act 1989 must be applied to CAMHSs.

The Health Advisory Service Review (NHS/HAS, 1995) proposed that child mental health services should provide an assessment service for an increased number of purchasers. The situated resistances to achieving this have been understated. The tendency to case possessiveness and the action-driven nature of the culture, will need very firm management to prevent assessment flowing seamlessly into treatment. Crucial changes in practice may, therefore, be demanded, and the endpoint to an assessment requires clear definition. These efforts will have to counterbalance the temptation in a world of too many referrals, for any purchaser to hand the case over for solution not just assessment.

Requests for 'assessment only' would have a most powerful and positive effect on the efficiency and effectiveness of child mental health services. It would:

- Increase the possibility that the 'special' and interesting, perspective of the child mental health agency would be shared more widely.
- Target and conserve a scarce resource.
- By undermining the monopoly, it would open up many other options for help.
- Offer a defined remit for audit leading to the development of an evidence-driven service.

At this midpoint, some themes are emerging:

- Within the case records more than one way of understanding the child's situation can be observed.
- Technical failure and resources influence the case trajectory.
- The agency is involved in social regulation.
- Very little is being said by children.
- There are both gains and losses, for the child, in an encounter with a CAMHT.
- There are continuing signs of poor collaboration.

The next chapter looks at the consequences of having a restricted gaze on to the world of the client.

Chapter V
LOST TEXT

(Roseanne 12.0) liked being at maternal grandparents more than home … urinary infections, mother has severe rheumatoid arthritis (frequently hospitalised). Diagnosis: Chronic anxiety tension state. Genetic factors? (Psychiatrist)

In the CAMHT, people worked independently of management and supervision from outsiders. This is the first of three chapters looking at the impact this can have upon users. Importantly, they show how accounting practices can diminish the client's voice and seriously disadvantage them. It bears repeating that this is a study of a subset (five per cent) of the work of the agency. It might be argued that whilst they are showing what happens when there are serious shortfalls in professional performance, this was not general to the agency.

Through reading records, it is possible to identify some of the processes of interaction and the subtext in an agency which will have a significant impact on decision making. Here it is shown that such 'lost' text can be recovered from limbo if either of the following can be identified:

- Anomalies and inconsistencies which weaken the assessment.
- Unambiguous evidence for different social constructions.

Much of this material was 'discarded' when converting the 'binary construction' to a singularity (Chapter IV). As will be recalled, in this process, interest moved from the child's life in the community to the child's emotional and behavioural state.

Smith (1978) deconstructed an interview with the flatmate of 'K', who in the former's view was mentally ill, and concluded that it was a:

Normal feature of accounts that they do not contain irrelevant material (and due to) lack of sufficient information any alternative account must be speculative. The construction of an alternative account in which 'K' is not mentally ill, is not possible.

Ibid., p.51

This ethnography provides evidence that in equally restricted accounts disconfirming elements were not erased but lying around and available for the reader to form into other ways of understanding the situation. The yield from the ethnography was so rich that it was not necessary to 'go back to the personages of the original to recover material that might be relevant to an alternative construction' (ibid.). This unexpected outcome was highly significant. Within the text was information of sufficient magnitude to at least question the sense being made by workers. Finding such 'alternative constructions' in a world where, as was shown in the first chapter, everyone concentrated on producing the same story, suggests that a less cohesive ideology will produce an abundance of 'versions of things' (Bateson, 1973). This is a gift to the performance assessor who can ask why certain narratives are preferred.

Alternative Constructions

One group of cases provided a most striking 'alternative construction'. Nearly eighty per cent of all the children (seventy-seven out of ninety-nine) were likely to have been the victims of 'sexual abuse' (Bagley and Ramsey, 1985; Rimsa et al., 1988). That there was, potentially, at least one other well-grounded way of understanding the young person's distress, challenged and undermined the discourse. The ability, to do this, simply from a textual analysis, was unexpected.

Using this analytical category to exemplify a 'hidden' social construction, had some attendant disadvantages. It was very much flavour of the decade (Bentovim et al., 1988; Olafson et al., 1992), and might be a 'faddish preoccupation' (Terr, 1989). Nevertheless, a rigorous and cautious approach which avoided second guessing assessors, produced a mass of seemingly unequivocal evidence. Three subgroups of this group of cases were generated. Groups one and two supported the argument most strongly:

1. Cases (eight out of ninety-nine) where the assessors were informed of prior actual, or alleged, sexual abuse.

Margaret (11.3):

Sex: There have been incidents when Margaret was allegedly interfered with by a man. The first had medical evidence to corroborate it ... The second seems more doubtful because conflicting accounts were given by Margaret. (Psychiatric social worker)

Claire (14.0):

Allegation that she had been sexually assaulted by mother's stepbrother. Police informed took no action. (Psychiatrist)

Irene (8.0):

Sexual assault by stepfather for which he was convicted. (Psychiatrist)

Marie (14.9):

Wrist cutting, stealing, smoking, swearing, truanting, absconding from children's home. Innuendoes were made that there may be an unnatural sexual relationship between mother and daughter. We have recently confirmed this with agreement from both ... Subsequently denied. (Psychiatrist)

Alex (10.2):

Wrote a note describing sexual intercourse, but not conclusive of sexual activity, pseudo adult behaviour, whining and clinging to mother, wants to sit on men's laps. (Psychiatrist)

Sue (14.4):

When she was seven school did not like the way he (cohabitee) allowed her to sit on his lap ... there was an incident where blood was discovered on the wall and pillow of Sue's room. Sue never said anything but (mother) began to distrust him. At eleven maternal grandfather allegedly pushed her up against some coat hooks making the back of her neck bleed and would not let go … At twelve, Sue asked to be taken into care … she was frightened that her grandfather was going to attack her again. (Community Social Worker)

Lorna (12.6):

Exhibited violent and frequent temper tantrums which neither mother or maternal grandmother could handle. Their previously peaceful house was in a permanent state of chaos and upset. Compulsive excessive and extreme public masturbation and smearing faeces 'truculent' rude and hateful to foster mother. (Psychiatrist)

Sally (14.6):

On the At Risk Register she alleged that her brother-in-law had sexual intercourse with her. (Psychiatrist)

2. Cases (forty out of ninety-nine) where substantial evidence emerged later in the life of the case. This happened most frequently once the children felt secure in their residential placement. (For example Rhian.)
3. Cases (twenty-nine out of ninety-nine) where the reader had little doubt that the child was the victim of sexual abuse. (For example Joy referred to in the previous chapter.)

Discounting Processes

The possibility of discounting an aspect of a child's life that could be emotionally, psychologically and physically harmful arose from restricted interests, medicalisation, and habit. This tunnel vision meant that text was lost. There were key places where this happened:

1. Referral:

Information was lost in the effort to interest the agency in taking the case:

Main problem one of disturbed family relationships and adolescence, but Sally could be disturbed in her own right and urgent psychiatric assessment needed. (General Practitioner)

2. Appointment talk:

Some clues and 'facts' being discarded in order to fit the agency business:

(Ruth 11.5) an only child. When I asked what they felt the problem was with her, mother said that she is most unhappy over school, but then it came out she can't face the night and she won't happily go off to sleep and is staying awake as long as possible, sometimes going to sleep on the sofa. She is now sleeping in her parents' room. (Psychiatrist)

Disturbed behaviour produced a focal point:

Ruth has been saying that she doesn't want to live any more and that there is nothing to live for. (Psychiatrist)

Focal points were then 'magnified' in the process of matching the child to the problem-solving technology. Education was the core business of the hostel:

History of complaints: Ruth has never liked school. At the end of last term she stated she never wanted to go again, she hasn't been this term and she is at present under the doctor and on medication, which father feels has produced slight improvement. She has always liked the academic side of school, it is the social side meeting the other children which she finds she can't cope with … Ruth gets very hysterical and says that nobody can help her. Ruth took some while to get used to leaving her mother. Ruth said that she would like to go to a boarding school. (Psychiatrist)

Material continued to emerge which would support suspicions regarding sexual abuse:

Ruth does still wet the bed from time to time. Father said that twice it has been rather upsetting when she went to sleep on the sofa and she wet herself as she woke up and this distressed her a lot. She has been a little easier since she had a bed in her parents' room. (Psychiatrist)

Even this account did not arouse any suspicion:

She never wants to go to bed and father either lies down with her or stays up and amuses her – for instance last night they stayed up and played cards until about two in the morning and then she goes to sleep. She sleeps very restlessly and talks in her sleep. Father said when they talk about bed she sits there staring and gets very tense and upset. (Psychiatrist)

Instead a picture of neuroticism was developed. Dogma was prevailing:

When I asked what habits she has, she apparently blows and sniffs a lot and picks her nose. She worries a lot over her hair and thinks she is ugly. She doesn't show a lot of affection to her parents. In fact, she can be nasty to them and blames them when things go wrong. She would like her daddy to be home more than he is. (Psychiatrist)

The scene was awash with over anxiety, mental vulnerability and social inadequacy:

This girl has always had difficulties coping socially with other children. Describes herself as timid but copes well with adults. She is an only child which may have some bearing on this. She has never been very keen on school. (Six months ago) she started at the convent, but (one month later) she was finding she could not cope with lessons and was getting frightened. She was also finding it difficult to get to school (and) out of the house on her own, feels everyone looking at her and feels panic. (Psychiatrist)

By this stage there was no suspicion that Ruth was experiencing sexual abuse, and opinions were forming about who was offering more appropriate parenting:

Mother has now moved into her room, and she has moved to the parents' room, sleeping in a single bed. This is because she wants to be with her father, who she finds, probably, more comforting than mother. (Psychiatrist)

Ruth had a story to tell:

She tells me that she gets very sad and depressed and worried about school, particularly at night. She feels that everything is pointless and she thinks about sad things. Apart from this, she wakes at about midday and has a ravenous appetite and has put on a stone in weight. (Psychiatrist)

Ruth was condensed to a bundle of worry:

At interview she was a very talkative, self-possessed eleven year old, who did not appear to be depressed, but who clearly is very worried about her future. I would suggest she continues on her present medication, and I have said to her parents that I would like her to be admitted to our inpatient unit for a period of assessment. (Letter from Psychiatrist to General Practitioner)

After ten months in the adolescent unit the portrait of 'anxiety' had generalised to all family members:

School phobia with anxiety states – enmeshed anxious family and associated problems caused by a highly anxious mother. (Psychiatrist)

Inadequate parental control justified separation:

And a father who has allowed his daughter to become too powerful within the family. Both parents are ineffectual in making her attend school. The best alternative is the hostel. Her peer relationships are difficult and she is ingratiating to staff, making her unpopular with her peers. (Psychiatrist)

What is striking is how apparently totally unaware assessors were that other social constructions were being excluded. (There was clear evidence that this did not arise from ignorance of sexual abuse and its sequelae (Olafson et al. 1992).) High levels of convictedness about the major storylines about emotional vulnerability reigned supreme. Following discharge from the hostel, Roseanne was advised by her psychotherapist:

> *All relationships contain problems, and the only really helpful thing is to stay with the problems and work your way through them – not run away to another person, and when this has problems go back to the other person.*

The cost for Roseanne was high. At eighteen, still living with her father, she was pregnant and chose not to reveal the identity of the father.

Displacement

Information was degraded if:

1. Opinions were voiced by non-professional people:

> *Foster parents had believed for some time that the uncle who lived with her maternal grandparents had an unnatural sexual relationship with Lorna, who they observed was excessively and unnaturally affectionate to him. There had never been any evidence for this at all. (Psychiatrist)*

2. If it was connected with another agency which could produce competing perspectives. In this example, Sally was on the child protection register. Sally was 'inflicting cigarette burns and cuts to her arms, and drinking to excess'.

> *History of the development of the problem between Sally and her mother. Mother had good relationship despite Sally being boisterous and difficult during infancy, until age eight when befriended a streetwise girl undesirable relationships with children from a local children's home. At ten she became flirtatious and uninhibited and boastful of how attractive she was to boys and men. Coincided with sister getting married and onset of puberty. (Psychiatrist)*

Dissociation from the formal interagency child protection processes left the CAMHT wide open to make dangerous interventions by omission or commission.

3. The dominant discourse overwhelmed competitive text.

Sally increasingly oppositional and has exploited her father's overindulgence and his failure to support his wife to discipline and control. Sally succeeded in splitting her parents up and getting her father to turn against her mother. (Psychiatrist)

There were two competing explanations for Sally's distress. The outsider's view that significant harm had occurred, stood in contrast to and was erased by the insider's proclamation that Sally was 'in her own right an exceptionally disturbed girl ... venomous when disciplined.'

Typically, the agency provided a readily available solution:

Father agrees that Sally has to stay away until all the problems have been solved. (Psychiatrist)

Information was selected which reaffirmed hypotheses:

We agreed that before she returned home, the family relationships would have to be on a sound footing at which Sally accepted her parents as parents ... they worked together in accord, and Sally's oppositional aggressive hostile attitude had changed. (Psychiatrist)

Even after eighteen months at the hostel, that team were still asking: 'What is so bad about Sally staying at home?'

A Hierarchical System

Rules of interaction play a part in restricting the focus of assessment and reducing opportunities to follow-up different matters. In this agency the distribution of power was hierarchical. Information, controlled at the highest level, created a vacuum in decision making. Chapter XI explores how interagency groups can ensure that a holistic approach is taken to casework.

The Psychiatric Social Worker was very suspicious that Rozanne was a victim of sexual abuse and said that Rozanne should not be left in the care of her father when her mother was in hospital. This advice was overruled because at interview with the psychiatrist Rozanne 'denied that she had said anything about sleeping with her father or asking questions about pregnancy.' Having ascertained the 'truth', the psychiatrist's attention turned towards 'agitated attention-seeking behaviour gaucheness and tics', and away from:

> Told a friend that she was sleeping with her father and might be pregnant. A joint police and Social Services investigation concluded that she was only in the same room. (Psychiatrist)

Hostel staff transferred information to fieldwork staff (Walton and Elliott, 1980). Five months before Amanda (15.6) was due to be discharged, the hostel manager ('warden') reported that Amanda had told a 'housemother':

> Her father touched her in the wrong places when tucking her up in bed and did not want to go home. She has been observed to cuddle and get physically close to him (in perfectly innocent way). Obviously the complaint is worrying but I feel at this point we can do no more than make people aware.
>
> She is seeing the psychiatrist regularly. We are unable to assess the significance of her remarks about father. Mother is out on night duty a lot but her behaviour with father does not suggest she is physically afraid or repulsed. Still rather infantile, cuddling, and naïve self-exposure.

Subordinates dipped a toe in the water, but quickly withdrew it:

> Placement at the hostel has proved relatively successful in that Sally has remained here and we have been able to get her home periodically. Attempts at family reconciliation have been thwarted by all three members. It seems there is some serious factor or factors unknown to us which lead to explosive breakdown whenever we seem to be getting some success. (Hostel Warden)

Hostel staff sometimes took courage from their close contact with the young people, and were prepared to keep their toes wet and not degrade the information:

> *I think it is significant that just before she is due to leave us such an explosion should have occurred again … Sally has continued from time to time to talk of abuse by her brother-in-law and to be angry when the family do not believe her. She continues to visit her sister. Sally has made these accusations during group at the hostel and then told her parents … Father's reaction was to become extremely angry and threatening towards her saying the problem is Sally causing the group leader (warden) trouble again. (Hostel manager)*

The conclusion was bold:

> *Her relationship with her father previously was grossly almost unpleasantly overprotective … I was very concerned about his attitude and wondered if he had been overinvolved with Sally. I wondered too why it is that Sally can only manage one or two days at home before a tremendous flare up between them all. (Hostel manager)*

The information and the evolving question fell into the abyss of the clinic, and there were no formal mechanisms to take the issue further. There were examples of more powerful tactics. Chloe (14.3) who had come to the residential unit because she was:

> *School phobic … overdoses, panic attacks, collapses, hypochondriacal and illness, conscious hysterical conversion symptoms. (Psychiatrist)*

Hostel staff produced a list of possible sources of harm:

> *Everyone within the team has at some point been involved in trying to get to the bottom of the problem to no avail and we have produced a list of possible causes:*
>
> - *Sexually abused by a man as she has complained that she was attacked in public toilets.*
> - *Abuse (by mother's cohabitee).*

91

- *Mum and her love bites.*
- *Phil – whose boyfriend? Mum's, Chloe's or both?*
- *Is mum prostituting Chloe?*
- *Worry of Aids.*
- *Is Chloe pregnant? The answer is no.*

Chloe wishes to have a urine test to see if she has an infection. She has also asked for a mild sedative. According to mother, her daughter is a very good actress. We do know that if we are to bring Chloe through the current crisis, a social worker will have to give mum lots of support. (Hostel manager)

There was no follow-up by the Consultant Psychiatrist. There were some constraints upon subordinate staff. Firstly, insubordination might jeopardise the continued use of the hostel because a Psychiatrist was the gatekeeper. Secondly, the intramural team was small and interdependent, which may have made it difficult to have disagreements. Thirdly, 'therapeutic work' was reserved for those who worked in the clinic environments. Carol Ann (14.2) showed behaviours that are typical of girls who have been or are being sexually abused (Rimsa et al., 1988). She was self-mutilating, 'cutting self arms and top of legs with razors'. Had taken 'an overdose' and was 'suicidal'. Carol Ann was admitted to the hostel:

Came in quietly and confidently. She says coming to the hostel was second choice. First choice was death. Says she is scared of all men – hates brother. (Hostel manager)

Halfway through her eighteen-month stay, Carol Ann told a housemother:

Of the sexual assaults that she had endured at school for three years. (Hostel manager)

This is as close as she came to disclosing abuse. The housemother had to leave further 'talk' to accredited clinic staff. This raised issues about policy and training (Utting, 1991; Walton and Elliot,

1980). Perhaps there would have been a weak response to demands to extend the role because, inevitably, this might challenge clinic assessments. To undermine the dominance of the psychiatric account would be like removing the keystone from the building that might then disintegrate.

This typifies contemporary tensions in relationships between residential and fieldwork staff (Kahan, 1994). Fieldwork staffs have claimed the right, largely by virtue of professional accreditation, to work with children and families in the community. The empirical findings support those who are pressing for an extended and more flexible role for residential workers (Cliffe and Berridge, 1991).

Summary

The narrowness of the assessor's field of vision was striking. Careful reading of case records has produced strong indications that other ways of construing cases can be found within text. This allows the evaluator to interrogate the text and perhaps find constraining mechanisms like the interactive patterns of the empirical world, which contributed to reducing the visual field. It is not being claimed that sexual abuse is the reason for the distress of these children. Alternative perspectives merely introduce the possibility that the way the situation is dealt with, the processes of interaction in an agency, and the outcomes for children and families should be closely examined. The importance of being able to suggest, albeit unproven, but persuasive alternative constructions afforded comment both generally and in detail on the social constructions and accounting practices of the agency. By extension for cases that are 'stuck', reviews should consider:

- The discounting processes (displacement, narrowing, transposition, magnification, condensing, blurring, and fit), which act to (dis) confirm a dominant viewpoint.
- How unpredictability and risk are managed.
- The processes of interaction and resolution of conflict.
- The quality of collaboration and interagency working.

'Stuck' cases are often peppered with jerky moves that fragment families and create situations which are hard to recover. These are illustrated using the case of Sonia in Appendix II. Resisting the switch into more detrimental interventions at crucial decision-making points, will demand that the social construction is reviewed, and perhaps, radically, altered. Supervision, that is appraisal by an outsider who brings difference to bear on practice, can produce such shifts.

Strangers in the Intramural World

What follows is a slight digression. When considering the possibility that some of the children were the victims of sexual abuse, the interaction of some of the men with parenting responsibility (potential abusers) with the clinic was striking. It stood out because of the marked marginalisation of male carers by the clinic. Their acts of sabotage, uncooperativeness, extreme intrusiveness, intimidation and dominance highlighted the inadequacy of the assessor's negotiating skills in situations of conflict and their lack of suspicion. There was evidence that male carers used their presence to exercise control over both the child and the assessors, and ensure that abuse was not revealed.

Silencing

It was highly unusual for fathers to attend appointments. Samantha (fifteen) who was 'heading for anorexia', came with her father:

> *Stopped eating and drinking, does not like school, academically strong. Jealous of brother, clashes with mother. Father says she has trouble showing affection and meeting people.*
> *Diagnosis: Severe anxiety tension state. Treat antidepressants. (Psychiatrist)*

One week later, father and daughter returned:

> *Moderate improvement ... Been to school. Would value father doing something special Treat day patient to assess the problem*

more fully and make a sensible plan for her future. My feeling is that this is not an educational problem but one of family relationships. Samantha is feeling very lonely and uncared for. (Psychiatrist)

Attendance by fathers was positively connoted. Sonia's adoptive father attended every interview and wrote six letters. He came to several interviews without his wife. His excuses for her absence included: 'It's getting to her' ... upset by Sonia's behaviour. Assessors became alert: 'could (wife) be being excluded by her husband?' but took no action.

Sabotage

Several fathers wielded control from afar:

Mother and Rhian depressed, downtrodden and angry mother gave glimpses of an intolerable home life and extremely difficult husband. He has forbidden his wife to come to the clinic and makes a great fuss if social workers and others call. (Psychiatrist)

Roseanne's father who was:

Very protective and attempting always to give reasons for her behaviour in order to excuse it, not explain it. Appears to be trying to keep her as his little girl, would not cooperate by attending the clinic. (Psychiatrist)

Rozanne declared she was 'in a mess and wants help to sort it out.' Perhaps her 'overindulgent and overprotective' father managed the consequent danger that she might reveal her situation by 'refus(ing) admission' to the adolescent unit. Sometimes the intrusiveness was striking, Jo (8) was:

Progressing well in psychotherapy, but father used to come and collect her at therapy time, so she missed a bit – father was angry at being asked to call a little later. (Psychiatrist)

There were the signs of inappropriate intimacy. Sonia's adoptive father reported:

> *That Sonia suffers from severe premenstrual tension and gets better when her periods start. (Psychiatrist)*

He oscillated between agreement with plans which required Sonia to live away from home, and fierce resistance and distress. He reacted to the loss of his 'child-wife' by asking the Psychiatric Social Worker to visit him at home so that he could:

> *Say how angry and upset he was about the care order as Sonia could not come home … 'I must have her. Could not come home, home.' (Psychiatric Social Worker)*

Speculatively, this was a case riddled with signs that father had an incestuous relationship with his daughter. Suspicion surfaced at the hostel:

> *Strange story of father going to Social Services' department to report that daughter had a lump on her breast. We are concerned that Sonia confides to her father that she has a lump on her breast. (Hostel manager)*

Sally's father succeeded in giving:

> *The impression that Sally had been an extremely disturbed girl throughout her childhood and that we should have seen her four years ago when she first began to show quite severe aggressive behaviour. (Psychiatrist)*

He convinced the assessor that:

> *Clearly the relationships between her and her mother had broken down. (Psychiatrist)*

To the reader, Sonia's adoptive father succeeded in preventing open communication and in continually undermining attempts by others to be helpful. By engineering private interviews, father managed to insinuate his explanations for the situation:

Father not sure if (adoptive mother) wants to maintain the family links. There is aggression between her and Sonia – (he said) 'perhaps they can't live together but they can still be friends'. (Psychiatrist)

He intimidated the assessor, and disempowered his wife:

'My wife, particularly, is finding her too much to handle and, as a result, spent the whole of yesterday in tears. I am not prepared to let the situation deteriorate to the point where she has a breakdown. She is not entirely rational all the time.' (Psychiatrist)

Perhaps the assessor and adoptive parent, both male, were vying for power in a relationship that was mutually seductive and conspiratorial.

In summary, male perpetrators were 'present' in a particular way: they were intrusive, controlling, and spoke for others. The behaviour of male perpetrators at child protection meetings can be observed to have similar characteristics. Practitioners must be alert for these behaviours in situations where it continues to be unusual to meet men. As working closely with all the carers in the child's world (DH, 1989(b), DH, 1995(a)) becomes commonplace, this will become less easy to detect.

This digression has demonstrated how textual analysis can produce empirically grounded findings applicable to practice and open up further lines of research.

Conclusion

Contrary to Smith's view (1978), texts are rich in material for alternative constructions. Records have 'added value', particularly in ensuring that work is of adequate quality. Attention should be paid to the assessor's 'story' (Hall, 1997) which will be more robust with:

- The accretion or deletion of material.

- The ability to quickly create enough material to form a basis on which to produce a solution.

Interestingly, even in a tightly constructed discourse focussed on children with problems, other constructions persist or resurface through time. Sometimes they are trapped in the interstices of other accounts like atoms in a molecular lattice, but they can be prised out. These alternative stories may at times have very faint signals, but, importantly, they have not been erased. As a consequence of this performance, there is a possibility that children were only partially protected from abusers who were free to continue to molest them, their siblings and other children.

The next chapter continues the exploration of the client's encounter with the agency by looking at the 'social regulatory' activity. This theme emerged in the study of the reasons for referrals (Chapter II), and featured strongly in all subsequent processes of interaction. The amount of disciplinary activity was surprising because the rhetoric concerned caring for disturbed children not controlling the deviant.

Chapter VI
GOVERNING CHILDREN

No real evidence of anything other than a fairly severe anxiety state with considerable hysterical and manipulative overlay. From bitter experience I have found that the only way that works with such children (Judy) is to deal with them in a very kind but firm way and try to put a bit of spine into the parents. This kind of girl does very badly if we are placating or reassuring. (Psychiatrist)

Child mental health services give the impression that they are benign providers of assessment and therapy for those with mental health 'disorders' (NHS/HAS, 1995). However, these records paint a picture of extensive social regulatory activity:

If we re-admit Judy, she will make a tremendous fuss and the operation will have to be carried out as quickly and smoothly as possible. As we will have to avoid argument with her, just get on with it. (Psychiatrist)

This chapter shows that the 'difference' between young people served by child mental health services and other agencies was defined by:

- The route chosen by referrers.
- The language used to describe their needs.

Consequently, many children could carry into adulthood a sense that they have fragile mental health (Nicholson and Ussher, 1992; Penfold and Walker, 1984). Unequivocally, most of these children (like Alex, Jasmine, Sandra, Judy, and Caroline) could have been managed by a number of agencies (Malek, 1991).

I should be grateful for your advice about the management of this very difficult girl (Kim) who is totally rebellious at home and difficult to handle in every way. (General Practitioner)

They were rarely 'mentally ill' but distressed by experiences of harm and deprivation.

At first I hoped that by working with mother we could effect an improvement. Alex's (10.2) conduct disorder continues unchanged and will do so as long as she stays at home where there is little affection and no control. She is an immature little waif. At school she causes grave concern with her cigarettes and make-up. (Psychiatrist)

It was the association with the 'medicine of tissues' (Foucault, 1977) that made the difference:

I (General Practitioner) have prescribed Diazepam to damp her (Kim) down.

'Underlying reasons', allusions to mental instability, 'is it inherent in her personality?' or medico-psychiatric matters, 'mother says that she will damage her brain' began to camouflage disciplinary activity.

Ellie (14.10) was suspended from school as a result of a:

Culmination of a series of incidents in which she refused to accept the school's authority, losing her temper and swearing. (Head Teacher)

Educational welfare matters were also readily accepted as legitimate work for the CAMHT. Acting like Social Services or Education Departments, it vacuumed up those whose challenging behaviour could not be tolerated in the community, rescued those in need of nurture, and re-established social order. When issues of social control were uppermost, records were often colloquial and only lightly sprinkled with psychiatric terms:

Alex's behaviour must reflect grave lack of care at home and would disappear if she were in a fairly secure and caring environment. The outlook without intervention is poor. (Psychiatrist)

Command and Control

I find it useful at initial family interview to conduct what amounts to a therapeutic trial of confrontation.

Framrose, 1978, p.356

Regaining an upper hand was catalysed by pridefulness and the need to preserve the agency. A patrician stance predicated on some primitive myths about girl children (Strong, 1985), precluded debate:

Sonia's alienation led her to seek friendships outside the family's control and to getting very early sexual experience and gratification, which increased her rebellion against her parents, who naturally wanted to protect her. (Psychiatrist)

Rebellious, disobedient girls who flouted the social mores risked becoming immoral. Such faulty relationships to the social world demanded repair. Angela (Chapter IV) was:

Manipulating everyone by announcing she was going back to school and then not. It came to the point where she was refusing to accept any control. (Psychiatrist)

Evaluating the work of an agency must take into account:

- the remit of other agencies;
- information about best practice; and
- the agency's priorities.

Warrant to make predictions justified intervention:

(Judy continued) As I see it, the only alternative will be a long chronic neurotic life. (Psychiatrist)

Talk of 'anxious', 'neurotic' and 'phobic' girls justified the prescription of a 'special' weapon – tranquillisers and antidepressants, 'to help her with going to school', 'to boost her confidence'. Medication was a powerful and rapid means of social control, a chemical cosh to alter mood, reduce 'argumentativeness', or 'to damp(en)' rebellion.

ILLNESS OR EXCUSES?

Assessors differentiated the biddable from the uncontrollable, the disturbed, or the deviant. 'Weak', 'silly', 'giggly' girls who were 'making excuses' and 'not taking things seriously' were distinguished from the sick 'intractable school phobic(s)' like Kate (13.0).

Fractionating naughtiness from neuroticism hid the muddle that prevailed. Disobedience justified issuing orders and threats. Neuroticism called for medicines and care. Either or both treatments diminished emotional distress and supported the resumption of education (Aldgate et al., 1991) which was a key measure of treatment success. The rhetoric deflected attention from the struggle between therapist and patient to achieve compliance. Kate typifies a pattern of treatment in the form of 'pressure of talk'. If 'x' does not happen, then 'y' will. The interactive sequence was:

1. a tranquilliser
A 'two-week programme of a step by step return to school.' (Psychiatrist)

2. Continuing 'talk'
After two weeks she was 'doing well'. (Psychiatrist)

3. Further commands
In the third week, Kate 'relapsed with PMT and abdominal pain' and failed 'to get in the morning at all'. In the afternoon she was 'only managing to hang up her coat'. A directive was given: if 'she was not taking the steps seriously and back to school by tomorrow', she would be admitted to hospital.

4. Separation
Kate was admitted to the adolescent psychiatric unit, 'angry and upset that her excuse had not been accepted'. (Psychiatrist)

5. Rehabilitation

Kate 'responded well' and was discharged after three weeks in hospital.

6. Repeat separation

For a week she went to school from home but then she had a 'sore throat' and was absent for a week. This 'hypochondriacal' behaviour was deemed an 'excuse.'

> *She agreed to go back to school on Monday or come into hospital. I hope that you (General Practitioner) agree that any non-contagious illness should be treated in (the adolescent unit) so that she can be got back to school as soon as possible. (Psychiatrist)*

The net was very tightly drawn. There was little evidence that children were enraged at the price they were paying for a situation that was beyond their control and built from nonsense.

A Physics of Intervention

> *'They (parents) try to control me. I (Sonia) don't want their discipline, morals, ways of doing things.' (Psychiatrist)*

Forces, pressures and resistances characterised interactions with wilful children. Sheila (14.3) had not been to school for three months:

> *Effort has been put into getting her back to school (by her parents). This she resisted violently at first but later she made some visits. Her resistance is not caused by fear but by a considerable degree of obstinacy that she was not going to do what adults told her – (Emphasis added).*

First some obstructions and reinforcing factors were removed.

DISPLACEMENT

Herbert (1978) wondered 'what to do with the rebel once all the usual methods of persuasion have been exhausted?' In the CAMHT, persuasion lasted a millisecond, then a battle of wills ensued. Parental 'permissiveness' allowed assessors to enter the fray and overturn 'weak' or 'ineffectual' parents:

Taking control out of their hands for this early school refusal in an early adolescent. (Jane) (Psychiatrist)

'Rebelliousness' was attributed to parental mismanagement:

(Parents) have no experience of this kind of difficulty and their intervention probably increased the alienation between themselves and Sonia. (Psychiatrist)

Patriarchal attitudes prevailed: 'father can control. We have a lot of confidence in him' and:

Dad should be supported in being in charge. Sonia was happiest when father was in charge of her and desperate when mother could not control her. (Psychiatrist)

'Inadequate' and vulnerable mothers were particularly easy to overpower (Chapter III). Penny (14.3) was 'highly unlikely to return to school of her own volition'.

I think it likely that Penny is uncertain about her relationship with her mother, and she has used her non-attendance as a powerful means of establishing a central role in the family. The consequence of Penny staying home is that (mother) has constantly had Penny as the focus of her attention and inadvertently has given Penny control of the situation through the use of a type of emotional blackmail. In my opinion, Penny has developed an ability to manipulate close relationships in a way that is damaging to both parties. (Psychiatrist)

A father who failed to provide 'secure and confident guidance and control to his family' (Skynner, 1974) produced children like Ruth, who had 'become too powerful', and Karen who 'controlled them in a maladaptive way'. In the families of school phobic children, fathers were described as 'passive, dependent and anxious', and 'competing for the maternal role' (ibid.). Karen's parents described themselves as 'highly strung'. Her father was discredited because he:

> *Would not let her ride her bike till she was twelve (… and he was) prissy, young and effeminate. (Psychiatrist)*

The assessors became cross and frustrated 'parents'. A programme of parent education is not considered, instead the child enters residential care (Chapter IX).

FIRM PRESSURE

Pressure of talk was applied in full measure once parents were deemed inadequate, collusive, or exhibiting the same mental pathology as the child. Lotte (1.4.9) had not been to school for three months, and her parents were, 'as with all these cases, very anxious themselves, and lack certainty'. This weakness provoked instructions to parents as well as their children. Two appointments, a week apart, aimed to remove the parental 'anxiety' which allowed children to be more assertive than their parents. The technique appeared to amount to nothing more sophisticated than a convictedness that the therapist knew best. Finally, a declaration of 'no progress' resulted in the child's removal from the family. (In this case it also overcame parental resistance to drug therapy.) 'Regular family meetings' continued at the adolescent unit, alongside:

> *Work on Lotte's social skills. Give her independence training and build her confidence before making a graded return to school. Mother like many anxious mothers is averse to medication. (Psychiatrist)*

No change was achieved even after eleven months:

> *The process of rehabilitation was prolonged, and required great pressure from us to overcome both Lotte's resistance, and the uncertainty and weakness of the parents. (Psychiatrist)*

Persistence on the part of the therapists and their power to asylum children meant that by one means or another, children would be compelled to conform:

> We put pressure on the family. Either Lotte return full time to (school) by the middle of the term, or she should be admitted to the hostel. As a result of this pressure, Lotte began to make an effort to return to school, but we asked the family to meet the staff of (a school serving the hostel) to discuss Lotte's options should she fail. (Psychiatrist)

RESISTANCE

Compliance was short-lived:

> Although Lotte managed school quite well and had attended full time, in the last month she appears to have lost her nerve, and all her difficulties of attendance have recurred. (Psychiatrist)

Temporary 'loss of nerve' was commonplace and called for a further dose of 'confrontation':

> Last week we repeated to the parents that either Lotte attend school normally, or she should be admitted to the hostel, as we see it as essential that she missed no further school in the last two years of her education. (Psychiatrist)

Adults ganged up against children:

> On this occasion, the parents showed great strength of mind, and when Lotte began to make a great fuss about attending school, they were strong enough to insist she go to the hostel forthwith. All agreed it was important they be given support about this, and an emergency admission to the hostel was agreed. Lotte went to (school) on the first morning after arrival at the hostel. (Psychiatrist)

Children could be formed, 'adjusted', and reformed with good enough parenting. The clinic, the hospital and the hostel were houses for the correction of deviance. Construed as places of rescue, they were in a marked way reformatories.

FORCE

Breaking action down into smaller parts and reconsidering patterns of interaction is a way of informing practice (and identifying areas for outcome study). Contrary behaviour initiated interactions that ranged from verbal threat to legal intervention. All this activity can be called 'force'.

THREAT

> *(Frances) school refuser, a very violent girl who has kicked in glass doors and windows, thrown radios, punched her mother (and needed) psychiatric treatment.*

Talking did not work, yet when Francis was admitted to the adolescent unit, she was 'orderly, sensible, and not suffering from any psychiatric disorder'. However, she 'failed the attempt to get her back to school from home.' Hostel placement was accepted as 'an alternative to court action'.

EFFORT FROM PARENTS

(Parents) 'must see that they have to be firmer for Angela's sake.'

INTERAGENCY COLLABORATION

> *Parents and school must be firmer in getting Angela there and not allowing her to use the sickbay. School counsellor to be involved. Staff must understand that her symptoms are the result of normal anxiety and do not stem from any physical cause. (Psychiatrist)*

Raising the stakes in the management of Penny went to unusual heights. An interagency strategy was proposed:

> *The options (for Penny)*
> - *Placement in a hostel attached to a normal secondary school as soon as possible.*

- *Joint action by Social Services and Education Department with a view to providing an alternative home base for Penny. (Psychiatrist)*

PLACEMENTS

Gail (11.8) had missed school for seven months:

Obstinate, resisting all attempts by school, myself (Educational Psychologist), and parents to get to school. (Psychiatrist)

Last term a 'home tutor tried to set up a desensitisation approach but she refused to go in the car'. At this point, Gail was admitted to the adolescent unit, for 'psychiatric assessment'. Six 'family sessions' occurred whilst she was an inpatient and:

Concentrated on giving the parental couple more authority and disengaging her from both her parents. It seemed that her anger at this happening gave her the impetus to return to school rather than accept a place at the hostel. (Gail was not) seriously disturbed. (Psychiatrist)

Following discharge:

The family (were) seen for a series of sessions to help with management of her more difficult behaviour and gradual return to school. (Psychiatrist)

Gail went to school for a while but then her parents 'could not persuade her to leave the house'. A new position was adopted:

Associated with relationships within the family rather than specific fears about school, although it is clear that after such a long time of absence, the return is likely to be a traumatic experience. (Psychiatrist)

This opened up a 'number of options':

1. Readmission to the adolescent unit, but this was opposed by Gail and her parents;

2. Prosecution of the parents for non-school attendance. This was set aside as 'unlikely to help the parents resolve the situation'.
3. A hostel place 'for further assessment and to ensure continuity in her education'; and
4. 'If Gail's cooperation cannot be gained, then an application for a care order should be made.' Gail agreed to go to the hostel.

At the end of her stay of twenty-six months, staff mused:

> *Something is still very wrong within the family – is father interfering with her? (Hostel manager)*

(This explanation for the children's behaviour was explored in Chapter V.)

LEGAL ACTION

> *Mother is deliberately keeping Charmaine at home for no apparent reason, and has done nothing to try and help her relate to her peer group. Slimming pills and diet have not worked. It needs much stronger action to help mother see the seriousness of the case. (Psychiatrist)*

Legal action overcame all resistance. Charmaine (13.6) was 'beyond her mother's control because she cannot get her to attend school'.

> *Seen today, mother says Charmaine has a sprained ankle and therefore cannot go to school. I have been seeing them (for eleven months). There were several failed appointments. We are wasting time and stopping more authoritarian agencies dealing with it. (Psychiatrist)*

The Social Services Department were summoned, and 'parental rights' were removed from her mother (Pre-Children Act, 1989).

A REBELLIOUS MOTHER AND DAUGHTER

This review of intervention strategies and outcomes raised many questions about their efficacy and ethics. The child with the most extreme behaviour shows how a double dose of 'non-compliance' (from Hollie (12.0) and her mother), triggered increasingly draconian responses. The early potential to manage the case in the clinic crumbled as both mother and daughter were deemed to have mental health difficulties. Hollie's Head Teacher saw things differently:

> *Difficult at school: refusing to bring her games kit; mood swinging from inattentive, rude and aggressive to good effort and concentration. She gives up easily. Hollie seems to change with the tide and act out many home pressures at school. We are not disturbed by her behaviour and can contain her outbursts.*

Mother and daughter 'displayed emotional and irrational outbursts with the teachers' (Nice, 1992). There was goodwill at school, and if hooking in to Hollie's mother's 'suicidal' talk had been resisted, and there had been close liaison with school, the course of events might have been different:

> *The problem for school staff is that Hollie is using her mother's unbalanced state to challenge the school's authority and avoid what she does not like. (Head Teacher)*

Hollie's mother was:

> *Depressed, withdrawn, peculiar and aggressive, very disturbed immature ... dictating how the interview should be conducted, refusing to speak. Walked out then hung round the door, looking paranoid, refuses psychiatric hospital admission. (Psychiatrist)*

Hollie's behaviour interested the agency:

> *Initially Hollie reacts in a paranoid negative way. Quite aggressive and assertive. Speaks for her mother who is behaving in a very inadequate, silent, unresponsive, withdrawn, resentful way. (Psychiatrist)*

A set of needs was produced which justified service provision from the CAMHT:

Diagnostic formulation: truancy and conduct disorder aggravated by her mother's mental illness. The model mother provides and the stress to which she exposes the children is the problem. Her son aged fourteen survives and shows appropriate social skills (he has respite foster carers). Daughter imitates her mother. (Psychiatrist)

Hollie was catching her mother's disease. Inexplicably, the dictatorial approach was set on one side in favour of a treatment plan that was kindly, and, surprisingly, simple:

Regular support, need positive reinforcement of their assets and no negative or critical remarks can be tolerated. Give them a good time here. (Psychiatrist)

After four months they stopped attending. Three months later Hollie's brother went into care at mother's request. The Community Social Worker described mother and daughter 'as the damaged damaging each other'. Hollie returned to the CAMHT as a 'school refuser':

A clear case for firm and immediate action. Mother who continues to be very paranoid, wants her in the hostel. Hollie is very oppositional. (Mother said): 'I'm not particularly fond of her'. (Hollie said): 'I've changed my name. I'm Jack the Ripper. I don't want to go into care ... I was adopted somewhere. She's not my Mum'.

Hollie was confronted with the options open to her (that is)

- *returning to school.*
- *going to the hostel.*
- *going to the inpatient unit.*

Initially Hollie refused to commit herself to any option. In consultation with (the Community Social Worker), it was agreed that recourse to law was essential to bring some control and security to bear upon Hollie, who was evidently distressed. (Psychiatrist)

When an application for compulsory admission to hospital or hostel was raised:

> *Mother threatened to break the psychiatrist's jaw and punch the social worker.*

Hollie was admitted to the adolescent unit on a Place of Safety Order (Children and Young Persons Act, 1969). Hollie ran away from the unit twice, and was very reluctant to move to the hostel. She was required to attend a court hearing for care proceedings:

> *The court case was delayed; Hollie was in contempt of court had to be taken to the cells to calm down. Eventually came back to the hostel. (Hostel manager)*

However, Hollie 'refused to cooperate', assaulted the Psychiatrist, and consequently spent twenty-two days in a regional secure unit. After discharge she stayed at the hostel for twelve months.

Extreme remedies for an apparently extreme girl. Hollie's 'school refusal and antisocial behaviour' provoked the full panoply of measures available. The saga points up the limitations of psychiatric treatment and the commonality with social work practices. It lends further support to the conclusion in the previous chapter that confining referrals to requests for assessment of need would prevent the CAMHSs applying their restricted range of remedies to inappropriate cases. An initial restriction to assessment only would highlight and enrich any different perspective offered by the CAMHS team and, therefore, clearly 'add to' the social constructions of others.

Conclusion

High levels of coercion were applied to children construed as wilful or victims of their emotional states. Rhetorical smokescreens hid essentially mundane work, which could, and in many cases should, be performed by other agencies. It suggests that an overinflated population of children (Rutter, 1973, 1975) receive a dose of child psychiatry. Catch-all phrases of 'emotional and behavioural disturbance' and 'mental disorder' mean that some children are being served by the wrong agency and may live with a sense that they have mental fragility. The importance of introducing a wide range of solutions into decision making has been demonstrated. As has the need to keep at the forefront of caseworkers' minds the need to apply the most appropriate, least detrimental, perhaps less expensive forms of support and protection (Taylor 2000).

Legal discourse has displaced the therapeutic discourses of medicine and social work (Parton, 1991) in defining harm to children, and the parameters of state intervention (Children Act, 1989). The principles, policies and practices that have accompanied these changes have not impacted fully on child mental health agencies. Yet, as has been shown, they are primarily engaged in the governance of children. Importantly the ethnography draws attention to a group of children and families who received services in an agency beyond the reach of the law (Chapter XI: Morris et al., 1980; Roche, 1989). Treatment options are restricted to in-house resources, and in consequence, children were and are being accommodated in hospital and residential units in the absence of the constraints and protections that policies and practice demand of other childcare agencies.

Cases were managed and problems solved by a series of transformations using in-house resources. The secret nature of the agency and its 'private remedies' allowed 'inaccuracy' in the social construction, the restricted compass of 'need' and the disinterest in the parallel services of other agencies to be obscured. These findings can be applied to the analysis of other organisations.

For practitioners the evidence in this chapter suggests that very extreme behaviour should be taken as a sign that not only is the child exposed to harm in the home, but perhaps is reacting to poor professional practice. The latter, as will be discussed later, can most certainly be 'adjusted'.

If the performance evident in this agency is found in other CAMHTs, then a rigorous refocussing and downsizing is called for. The evidence is building towards the final conclusion that it is time, either to reconstruct a clearly defined, contemporarily appropriate space in the universe of agencies for child mental health services, or none at all. The exploitation and oppression of children who will accept anything rather than responsibility for breaking up the family or losing their place within it was saddening.

The next chapter considers their plight in more depth.

Chapter VII
UTTERLY POWERLESS

'I sad' (Linda 10.0).

'I'm (Ruth 11.7) timid, sad, depressed about school, and especially at night. Everything is pointless and I think about sad things. I never want to go again. I can't cope with meeting other children.'

The voice (Millman and Moss Kanter, 1987) given to the children in the empirical world was very weak. They appeared powerless, their voices unheard. After describing some processes that led assessors to be oblivious to children, consideration is given to how children try to be heard, but appear to be silent and how they detect ways of making themselves safer. These are findings for application in practice. Finally, the idea re-emerges that a hermetically sealed universe, constrained by strict rules of confidentiality did not make children feel totally safe.

A World That Did Not Listen

None of the areas of difficulty identified by Sonia's referrer were thoroughly addressed by the CAMHT:

> *I (Educational Psychologist) see three main areas in which much more information and work needs to be done: her adoption, the relationship with her adoptive family, and her feelings about herself.*

There was marked inattention to 'external' matters like race, gender and culture (Williams, 1989):

> *Sonia told (her extramural worker) she was proud of being half Indian, but I wonder if in fact she sees it as somewhat of a stigma because she referred to herself as a coloured baby that no one would*

want to adopt, and she found it difficult to understand why her adoptive parents had chosen to adopt two half coloured children. I therefore wonder if Sonia has deep-seated anxieties about her mixed race, or whether this is a false impression much discussion should take place as to how Sonia's self-esteem can be built up so that she believes she is a wanted and accepted person. (Educational Psychologist)

After referral, these matters were 'forgotten'. The child's world was subcutaneous. Consequently, for example, difference between the gender of worker and child was not considered. It was probably not insignificant that Sonia's referrer was female, 'the interview was a long one because she clearly liked to talk' (Educational Psychologist*),* nor that children spoke to the female care staff at the hostel. Sonia began to menstruate at eleven and a half, her 'physical development was advanced'. The interview environment with a male assessor and parents present contributed to puberty and sexuality becoming a 'lost text' (Chapter V).

It is ironic that a specialist arena for vulnerable children could not in the main make meaningful contact with them. Children sometimes said something to extramural players:

The central problem seems to surround her feelings towards her brother Finlay and the possible great jealousy she has there. (Educational Psychologist)

Children were 'seen' and not heard, due to a preoccupation with connecting challenging behaviour to emotional states. Although the contribution of family life to children's 'disturbance' was acknowledged in the 'binary construction' (Chapter IV) and 'family work', the main interest was always measuring the mood of child.

Assessors appeared perplexed when young people did not articulate their troubles, 'it seems that she (Sally) had a real problem in communicating her distress in any other way than through rages.' Both silence and challenging behaviour were seen to be abnormal:

Rhian (15.2) withdraws from painful situations and fends off concerned people. Very sensitive about her family circumstances, which prevents her living life to the full … home is a bit disruptive for her. (Psychiatrist)

Rhian needed to toughen up and stop resorting to troublesome and life-threatening behaviour. Her 'histrionic and emotionally labile' behaviour (including overdosing) would, with 'psychiatric treatments' have a 'Prognosis: fair, likely to improve' (Psychiatrist). It was the child's responsibility to make the 'problem' clear to the assessor. Artwork (for an example see Appendix I), produced by the children during interview, was kept on file but how this was used, if at all, was unclear.

Sonia (fourteen) was unusually vocal. Her speech during an outpatient session may have been noted because there were court proceedings:

> *'They do the same in a children's home as in a family. There is not the emotional tie – I don't like any sort of tie. Family, that is. I hate it I don't want to know about it.'*

> *'I'm my own person I don't belong to anyone. They own me try to control me (weeps …) I have to say I love them … I don't want a home. I just want to be left. I don't want anyone to look after me. I just want to do it myself. The Social Services are better at looking after me'. Wants to leave and gets very distressed when we talk about love – when did you stop? 'I didn't have to come here. I don't have to take anything from anybody.'*

Pathologising behaviour permitted helpers to manipulate situations without hearing children's points of view. It was only after admission to hospital that staff began to hear about the difficulties of life at home:

> *She revealed that she was extremely unhappy about her relationships at home, and with girls at school. She was afraid to express how she felt. (Psychiatric Nurse)*

After sixteen months in the hostel, Sonia had still not disclosed anything. Staff said that she 'had a lot of very sad feelings that at present she is unable to share with us.'

Listening is sometimes painful and can make workers feel useless:

> *We tried to work with her parents but found the family*
> *relationships almost unbearable. Father is a very disturbed and*
> *difficult man who gets into violent and difficult rages if not getting*
> *his own way. He does not work. Mother takes the burden but is*
> *completely estranged from her husband, and would leave home but*
> *for the children. (Psychiatrist)*

One response was to rescue them by using the residential facilities. Rhian's:

> *Personality difficulties are likely to continue for a time, but I think*
> *it will now be possible for us to help her become a freer and more*
> *outgoing girl. (Psychiatrist)*

Children's Communication

Children picked up the cues and clues provided by workers. Here, in the presence of her parents, Sally hooked into interest in her relationship with her mother:

> *Sally feels the main problem is between herself and her mum.*
> *'Mum only likes younger children. She gets rid of them when they*
> *grow older. Wants me put in a home. Mum rules dad. He's afraid*
> *of her. Why should I always have to change? Mum needs to change,*
> *too. If she won't change, neither will I.' (Psychiatrist)*

Children gained power by 'drip-feeding the discourse' and trying to be heard using 'silent', 'oblique' and 'direct' forms of 'hinting'.

SILENT HINTS

Silence was construed as 'insensitivity', 'lack of awareness' or 'petulance', not as an active means of communication. Christine, (who was possibly abused by her brother over a number of years), was described as a:

> *Quiet girl who showed very little emotional response to the family*
> *discussions of her school refusing, and her home behaviour.*
> *(Psychiatrist)*

Unfortunately, these attempts to maintain composure allowed assessors to measure mental well-being.

OBLIQUE HINTS

Oblique hints were likely to achieve safety, even though they were incorrectly interpreted. Not going to school was behaviour that children found rapidly enervated adults. Corrective interventions were threatened if a child did not alter their behaviour.

> *(Sally) has period pains at night. 'Dad gets up to see to me. It's mum's job but she won't talk to me.' Parents won't believe her allegations against brother-in-law (of sexual abuse). She has retracted, hoping she will get on better with her parents. Apart from rows, she thinks she behaves well. She doesn't go wild with boys and works hard at school. She doesn't want to go to a hostel or boarding school or adolescent unit. (Psychiatrist)*

When Sally was seen alone, she chose not to say how she felt about father's behaviour, but used an oblique way of complaining:

> *'Mum answers back, I answer back, I don't treat her like a mum she doesn't treat me like a daughter. I would try but my mum wouldn't. What do you think I feel like when I have terrible period pains and no one looks after me? I hate her. I'll split them up somehow. I'll get her back.' (Psychiatrist)*

Sonia, and Rhian, hinted at sexual abuse by their adoptive father, and father, respectively, by accusing a brother and a brother-in-law. This did not work because it was taken literally, and in the absence of concrete evidence, discounted.

DIRECT HINTS

Some hints were metaphorical (Barker, 1985), 'I feel I have been beaten by my whole family' (Annabelle) or were announcements that sound true: 'Mum wants me in a home'. These bolder voices with an accusative tone conveyed the emotion attached to other experiences. Sonia maintained a storyline over many years that she was rejected. This was a real aspect of her situation. Roseanne hinted in a mixture of ways. She presented herself to helpers:

'Demands time from school counsellor but cannot use it', and made direct appeals: 'I'm in a mess and want help to sort it out'. There were other clear statements:

> *(Sonia 14.5) I have thought about our relationship and future together as a family. I don't feel happy enough within myself to cope with staying with you. When I have finished growing up within, I will get in touch. I love you both. (Handwritten letter)*

A few children asked for removal from home:

> *(Angela 13.11) I don't want to go home. I'll only be all right when they have sorted themselves out. (Handwritten note)*

Voices became bolder once the children were in the residential placements. At the hostel they could have partial safety until they left school at eighteen. They felt safe and gained considerable support from the regular, closed, 'group meetings'. Here they heard their peers talking about similar experiences and feelings (Barker, 1974). Nevertheless, some young people longed to be back at home. When Paula (12.0) was in the hostel, she wrote:

> *When I was five I started to wet myself I have seen many doctors and specialists. They don't know what is wrong with me. I've even been in hospital a few times for my problem. I don't know why I do it. I am worried about being away from home.*
>
> *I want to cure myself. I want to be normal. I can't stay here much longer. When I went home for the first time, I got very upset because a weekend does never last long and I wish it lasted for ever and ever. Every weekend I went home and came back on a Monday morning by hospital car. I really loved it at (adolescent unit), it was like a kind of hospital but I was allowed home even though the people were rather Scilly (sic) and they were mostly boys. They were my friends. The girls were like tomboys. I liked it at (adolescent unit). Within a week I liked it very much. (Sic).*

Some children had to get 'very upset' to alert a world that did not listen:

(Cont.) I find it very hard to talk to people about my problems and the first weekend I had to stay at (adolescent unit) I had a fight with this boy I got very upset, so a nurse that was new there she came the same day as me, she took me into a little room and I was so upset that I just told her everything about myself. After that I found I could speak to her but she was only training to work as a nurse. I carried on learning to speak to her, then one weekend my mum told me about the hostel (Sic).

There is strong evidence that children confide in people they trust. Those selected are often relatively powerless and may lack formal qualifications. This supports the recommendation (Chapter XI) that professionally qualified staff should not numerically dominate services.

The Origins of Hinting

Not speaking is often construed as self-protective. The ethnography shows that children are like 'radios', tuned to receive wavelengths that carry problem-solving information. From their early encounters with service providers, they detect ways of achieving at least partial rescue from their abusive situations. When assessors were in social regulatory mode, children were told what would happen if they did not alter their behaviour. Children heard these solutions and silently pursued them. Rhian was given a clue about how to gain safety without having to reveal her father's abusive behaviour. She heard her mother:

Advised to get in touch if daughter gets more depressed or suicidal, or is having difficulties at school. Educational Psychologist to be asked to keep in touch with school counsellor so that we have a warning system in school. (Psychiatrist)

A way out of her predicament was to act as a 'mad' or 'bad' person. A few weeks later Rhian asked to see the Psychiatrist by herself. Her teacher reported she was 'worryingly depressed'. Rhian's message to the Psychiatrist carefully encapsulated her dilemma and that of all abused children, to speak out or not:

Stays silent but not resentful, and when asked if there is some trouble, she looks down and flushes and looks about to cry. Does not deny wants to see me and when pressed says, 'I don't know'. (Psychiatrist)

This bid to achieve rescue did not quite work, so four days later Rhian 'overdosed on mother's tablets'. Rhian had heard the earlier injunction to become depressed or suicidal, and finally 'escaped' into hospital.

Children, many it is suspected with terrible secrets, did not have to speak. A lifeline was thrown unwittingly in talk directed to parents but in the presence of children.

Making Choices

The observation that children were listening out for a means of rescue is a profound one. Instead of concentrating on obtaining 'disclosure', practitioners might work from the premise that this is not an option for many, probably most children because they do not want to leave their family or carry responsibility for fragmenting it. Two practice tactics are useful:

1. Inform children that the therapist knows that some children are in dangerous situations, and that they can to differing degrees offer protection. The options can be outlined, with acknowledgement of any specific limitations to the level of protection that can be afforded.
2. Announce that work with the client will be 'as if' they had said that they were a victim of abuse. The child can then begin to make choices from a stronger position, irrespective of whether they are prepared to risk talking about what is happening.

From this evidence, treating children with respect and recognising the considerable abilities of quite young people to work a way through this is vital (Brimblecombe et al., 1989). CAMHSs must be evaluated to see how far children's decision-making capacity is distorted and undermined by the discourse about mental ill health.

A Clue to Treatment Failure?

Generally, soon after admission to hospital, the child's main 'symptoms' resolved. So, children who had not been attending school for many months, even years, went regularly to the education unit in the hospital. However, they foundered when they were reintroduced to their school of origin. Even Karen (14.2) was perplexed:

I want to go back but I cannot get there. I want help. I don't want to leave home … I want to be left alone.

Samantha's hospital treatment included:

Individual psychotherapy (and) family groups. Seen regularly to try to resolve some of their conflicts … It has proved impossible to get her back to school from home. Self-inflicting cigarette burns, cuts to her arms and drinking to excess at home. Samantha said that she was unable to return to her old school due to family problems. (Psychiatrist)

Samantha provided the clues and illuminated the behaviour of many of her ethnographic sisters. She refused to return to her school and family, and wanted at least partial rescue from her father's sexually abusive behaviour. Unusually, placement at the hostel did not instantly modify her behaviour:

Returned from the first weekend home with new burns. Complained could not see (admitted to hospital for two nights) then ran away from school. (Hostel manager)

Samantha was using a mix of oblique and direct hints in order to protect herself:

I ran away from school because no one seemed to be getting the message about how bad I was feeling and how much I hate school. I also want some time to myself to think about things. Dad hits and humiliates me in public. (Psychiatrist)

The concerns of her substitute carers escalated in response to talk about emotions and not going to school. These matters were their bread and butter:

> *She appears to dread and worry about contact with parents. (Hostel manager)*

Samantha won a decrease in home leave, 'To go home once or twice each term.'

Children in temporary placements who resurrect problem behaviour are indicating that their home environment continues to be unsafe. Unfortunately, their behaviour is interpreted as seriously disordered and requiring further treatment rather than just an expression of their wishes and feelings about returning home. This finding is ironic. The children were partially protected by the placements, but the accounting practices that achieved this were a charade. So there were costs as well as benefits for the children:

PARTIAL PROTECTION FROM ABUSE

The hostel offered shared care during term time only. Unless the involvement and vigilance of an agency inhibited the abuser, the child was not fully protected. After eighteen months at the hostel staff were perplexed and critical of shortfalls in clinic practice:

> *Samantha (16.6) 'won't stay home for the odd evening'. What is so bad about staying at home? An area we have not fully explored. We have never received a proper social history. We are completely lacking her early life. (Hostel manager)*

Despite these gaps in information, and Samantha's protestation 'they will end up murdering me,' she went home for the school holiday.

STIGMA

Varying degrees of stigma were experienced (Aldgate, 1989). Carol Ann said:

> *At my other school I was happy, loud and friendly. Here (hostel),*

I'm quiet. One girl asked me why I'm always in a shell. I'm withdrawn. What the hell is wrong with me? I've got this label round my neck. It says (name of adolescent psychiatric unit), so I'm classed as looney or ex-looney. I don't know what keeps me going.

Rhian (15.2) summed up the conflict:

I want to be put away because I'm mad. No! No!

CARRYING BLAME

Most children saw themselves as responsible for the situation, 'I hit mum and was naughty' (Tracey 11.10). Others actively volunteered to resolve it:

I'd (Alison 11.10) be willing to go into hospital if it is going to do something, because I keep upsetting my mum and (sister). I felt as if I wanted to be good. I don't know what made me go all haywire.

Blame, stigma and loss are costs children are prepared to bear. Anything rather than carry family breakdown or rejection as a legacy of their behaviour:

I (Judy 13.8) shouldn't have been born. My parents think I am a mistake and say I was trouble since the day I was born … Grown-ups seem to forget that they were young once. I want to be put in a home. The worse thing that could happen to me is to know that my parents don't want me anymore.

Summary

In the CAMHT:

- Power was vested in adults to determine what was 'wrong' with the child.
- The practitioners could not help the children make the required transition from behavioural to verbal expression.
- The quality of the talking therapy service (the appointments) was not reviewed partly because of the presumption that the

children did not speak because they were disturbed.

- The assessors magnified a few matters and erased most others.
- The exclusion of outside agencies removed the possibility of using less detrimental helping strategies.
- The absence of an arguably more accurate understanding of the child's situation, combined with insufficient interagency collaboration, meant that some children only received partial protection from harm.
- Children's readiness to accept blame was exploited.

CONFIDENTIALITY OR PRIVACY?

Confidentiality (GMC, 1991), privacy and rights 'are interwoven with a complicated series of debates and initiatives in theology, ethics, the law, social science, medicine etc' (Rojek et al., 1988, p.129). Total secrecy was a highly sought after feature of the agency:

Throughout my discussions with mother and Ellie (14.4), it always felt as if Ellie needed someone to talk to in her own right. For whatever reason, it seemed she rarely had a forum in which to voice her feelings, outside her home. Nevertheless, her actions have made sure she has been the focus of our attention. (Head Teacher)

The 'individual session' was an inner sanctum of the 'clinic':

I feel Sally (14.6) needs a separate person to whom she can talk and gain some understanding of what is really happening in Sally's mind. Questions that come to mind are: was she really sexually abused, and by whom? Perhaps not brother-in-law? Even if she is not, why does she have to keep bringing it up? She is a very jealous girl. Is it because she is very jealous of her sister's children and the care that is lavished upon them by her parents? (Community Social Worker)

To the therapist, Sally was:

A very brittle young woman who has cultivated a tough image. The more she talked about things that upset her, the angrier she got. It seems that she had a real problem in communicating her distress in any other way than through rages. I suspect her self-esteem is pretty low ... three further meetings with confidentiality assured are planned.

After:

Four sessions, hostile throughout, unable to see (female therapist) as helpful. Frightened to share feelings of vulnerability about past or future. Seemed worried it might stop her getting home.

Many children were in such dreadful situations, apparently quite misunderstood by assessors, that it must have compounded their 'rage' to be placed in 'therapeutic environments' that compelled them to hang on to their distress:

She (Sally) only occasionally let me see beyond her tough exterior. Nevertheless, we were able to address her hostility and possible reasons for it, and she may feel able to take up my offers of help to make sense of what has happened to her in her family in the future. (Psychotherapist)

These outcomes challenge the effectiveness of a milieu of strict confidentiality in work with children. It gives kudos to the actor but does not make the child totally confident that they will be safe in the long term. The Children Act 1989 is trying to hold a middle ground, seeking respect for rather than the strict application of confidentiality:

Everyone should respect the rights of adults and children to confidentiality over their personal affairs. On the other hand, adults and children need to know what information is held about them and what may be done with it.

DH 1989(b)

This is not rigorous enough to overcome the sanctity accorded to confidentiality in some organisations. Confidentiality is dangerous because it excludes other agencies, and their information, and important members of the child's extended world. The rule of confidentiality can be used to avoid interagency work, difference of opinion, and conflict of interest. Of itself, confidentiality cannot overcome the need for self-protection. Consequently, the actual or potential harm to children cannot be managed safely in a milieu of confidentiality.

Confidentiality in child protection investigations is always limited, particularly if they are subject to statutory intervention, and/or if the child is a witness in court (Ryan and Wilson, 1995). The evidence suggests that therapeutic work should be treated similarly. I have concluded that there can be no confidentiality in matters concerning children (Hoghughi, 1988).

Many children greatly valued the experience of consistent interest from workers, often over extended periods of time. Where this service is offered, children need information about:

- The limits of the workers' respect for the child's privacy.
- The ability of adults to cope with their information, nothing is too terrible.
- The levels of protection that can be afforded to them in a range of circumstances.
- What is negotiable and what is not.
- The advantages and disadvantages of talking about certain matters. For example, if they might lose contact with all or any of those who are significant to them (this extends beyond family to include school, peer group, and so on).
- The dilemmas and uncertainties that accompany any changes. (Because these cannot be erased, some children will still choose to give little away.)

These elements of child-centred practice can be achieved using age appropriate methods for individual or group work. Peer 'buddies' might help children make choices, rehearse the information they will share, and provide advocacy. A mind-mapping exercise with a group of young people would identify the range of information child clients need, and suitable publicity material could be created.

In summary, information should be treated as private, and sharing it on a need to know basis, mandatory (Chapter X). Confidentiality is obstructive and complicating, and the justification for it is thin (King and Trowell, 1992; Ryan and Wilson, 1995). It binds actors into conspiracy and is an excuse for keeping practice and decision-making secret. Mutual respect for the conservation of information must suffice and clients should know the rules by which everyone is working. A textually mediated shift from secrecy to 'privacy' – that is freedom from public attention – must be accomplished.

Conclusion

This was a world that concentrated on the message not the messenger. Particular features of the 'medicine of behaviour' excluded realities in daily living, especially 'objectification', infantilisation, and overcomplicated, narrowly determined, social constructions. The wide range of fears, worries and challenges that can face developing young people were invisible (Coleman, 1990). Failure to appreciate that some children might be dealing with adult issues did them a great disservice. It probably meant that Sonia had to protest a story about rejection, and dislike of her brother, in order to be partially rescued from the abusive behaviour perpetrated by adults within the family. Common and uncommon matters were made unimportant: from being bullied and teased because you are fat, and enjoy school work (Lotte), to the early onset of puberty, and a different skin colour (Sonia). This disinterest in matters of profound interest to children, meant that they entered an alien culture. The restricted compass of the assessor's 'gaze' disconnected the client from their environment.

Key factors that silenced children included:

- The CAMHT's early processes of donating meaning to the situation, and consequently gaining control.
- The CAMHT's disinterest in the child's outer world.
- Not talking to or listening to children.

In combination, these led to a pervasive neglect of the child's world.

The rule of confidentiality did not counter this power imbalance. It merely served to govern the distribution of power in the system. In their silence children were actively seeking a way out of their situation. Greater appreciation of and respect for this 'business' of distressed children might protect them from the excesses of dogmatic professionals.

Another practice point to highlight is that careful thought must be given to what is said to parents in the presence of children. Such conversation can be used wittingly. I do this in child protection meetings attended by young people where the carers deny the occurrence or likelihood of significant harm. It is made clear that the professional system disagrees with the carers and will be working to keep the child safe. Children, as has been shown, will hear what is said and may exploit what they detect to gain protection.

At this point, the ethnography has produced evidence that the extension of the contemporary critique of adult mental health services to the arena of child mental health services is vital. For the majority of children, to construe their behaviour as mental ill health is to miss the point and misdirect the efforts. If children's services resound with the voice of children, they are more likely to be working to a closer approximation of the source of their distress. Measurement of the quality of these services should be based on how children's wishes, experiences and needs are determined. Children in the empirical world have indicated that 'helpers' are those who are accessible, pragmatic and honest (England, 1986). Therefore, services must cultivate and cherish these workers.

Shifts away from a solution-oriented welfare culture will have huge political consequences. Aside from undermining institutions that thrive on blame and punishment, it will demand the creation of a child-oriented society. The construction of adequate preventative services has failed. However, the foundations for this movement can be built if common agreement is reached that:

- All child welfare agencies and organisations carry responsibility for addressing children's distress.
- Children are not innately a problem nor (with rare exceptions) do they have behaviour problems because they are mentally ill.

It bears repeating that children's behaviours are an expression of how they feel, a way of gaining something, and a product of their interactional experiences and environment. They also have a more limited and predictable repertoire of behaviour through which to communicate than adults. This is partly determined by their developmental stage and level of dependency, and mainly by the world in which they live. Not going to school is a ready way for a British child to indicate that all is not well. Therefore, it is predictable that they will 'use' it as a means of protest. This is not to imply that these actions are always volitional. School attendance demands an emotional energy that may be drained by abuse, lack of care or multiple other pressures. Importantly, the specific form of behaviour is less relevant than the message it carries: it is a signifier for distress. For many children their behaviour is designed to maintain secrets, or avoid family fragmentation, or deflect attention, and achieve some change. Practitioners would do well to make this a tenet of their work.

The next chapter provides compelling evidence which supports the changes in legislation and policy that have been designed to produce 'needs-led' practice. Importantly, it provides empirical evidence that the weaknesses of welfare technologies have an equally significant impact on the production of resource-driven assessments and therapies. To move closer to achieving 'needs-led' services, organisations must first address poor performance in both assessment and interventions designed to improve the service user's situation.

Chapter VIII
ALTERING TEXT

I will assess Alex for a term before deciding if the only hope is to get her away from home, for at least a part of the time, at our hostel. (Psychiatrist)

Judgment-making activity is a mechanism for transforming complex human situations into soluble technical problems. In the absence of restraints, the judges in this social world have little compunction about applying drastic strategies to bring about change. The move to a new form of provision obscures any technical failure in the assessment system. Examining the decision to provide residential care shows why we should evaluate the quality of the preceding work before users are exposed to major changes. Evaluation can point up the costs to consumers, and the benefits to assessors and providers of making a significant change in service provision.

The penultimate Chapter X will suggest how workers and interagency groups can evaluate their own performance.

This chapter demonstrates how an auditor can approach a professional world to enquire:

- What makes transformation in service delivery possible?
- What are the consequences?

It will be argued that a move to reflective practice (Schon, 1991) would minimise the level of intervention and allow more clients to remain at home.

Inadequate Technical Performance

Social text is primarily about negotiating the social world in order to survive it. This requirement frequently results in more detrimental and expensive interventions. Insufficient attention is paid to the effectiveness of professional practice on a case by case basis. Whilst in a sense it is completely obvious, practitioners rarely acknowledge the inadequacies of their techniques, let alone acknowledge it as a feature of situations (Parton, 1998). It has taken the hefty clout of official inquiries (Blom Cooper et al., 1995) or research (Vernon and Fruin, 1986) to uncover some inadequate practice. It may be helpful to tease out why when major interventions are recommended, a re-evaluation of the quality of past services is not standard practice. Granted this is partly because there is a pervasive culture of blame and it is, therefore, a delicate procedure to implement. One of the key tasks for agencies is, therefore, to counter the victimisation of practitioners, to praise their efforts, and to recognise the dilemmas and challenges that they face. Introducing performance appraisal at this early point is important because without interruption, some case trajectories are fairly unstoppable. Lorna's (12.3) maternal grandparents':

> *Capacity to change the way they handled her was limited, and they found the interviews rather difficult. (And on that basis they) accepted my offer of the hostel. (Psychiatrist)*

Such rapid transitions from one form of service to another might be halted following reconsideration of, for example:

- The quality of the worker's interview technique.
- The carer's capacity to change.
- The carer's commitment to the child.
- The service user's views.
- The user's willingness to continue with interviews in the light of the alternatives.

There are a number of components that distract attention from the quality of the professional work.

IRRECONCILABLE VIEWPOINTS

Lisa's parents consistently held that she was:

> *The cause of all the problems at home and are reluctant to face the tensions and difficulties in the relationships between all family members. (Psychiatrist)*

A major transition point occurred when the adult family members refused to be co-opted into the way the assessors construed the situation and would not participate in therapy. The conversational technique (talk) could not be used unless there was mutual agreement that the situation involved everyone and not just the child. Whyte (1997) suggests that workers should try and ally their construction as closely as possible with the consumers in order to initiate dialogue. Such collusion would stop the agency from making a 'difference'. The empirical evidence shows that it would invariably isolate the client with the problem.

There was a clash of perspectives about Jane (13.5) who because of her 'sore leg, inability to sleep (and) period trouble,' was absent from school. The assessor considered that her mother was colluding, but Jane's parents thought that her 'early school phobia' had its origins in life at school. Despite several meetings, the disagreement continued:

> *I suggested perhaps Jane was fantasising and fearful of something happening at home, and perhaps that was why she stayed at home. Jane's parents were defensive. Mother said that she was too immature (13.5) to have such concerns. (Psychiatric Social Worker)*

This situation cries out for conciliation. Assessors were seriously disadvantaged by the 'problem affirmation' that accompanied referral (Chapter II). Almost inevitably, in the absence of mediation skills, this undermined their work. Here there is also a stark clash of perspectives. An independent observer might suggest that in these cases attempts to suggest that the child's problem arose from marital or family conflict almost invariably failed, resulting in a difficulty in negotiating some common ground with parents. Perhaps conceding that more than one thing could be true at once, would overcome the resistance to cooperative working. There are three practice issues at this point. Firstly, to enter this debate would be complicated at a point when assessors were striving for order and simplicity, secondly, a concessionary strategy alters the balance of power in favour of parents, and thirdly, workers are inflexible and do not seem to have a variety of skills and techniques to apply.

Conflict in the family continued. Jane was:

Waking in the early morning complaining of headaches, but her mother would not permit father to get her up for school; 'not with his nerves. He needs to go to work relaxed'. The parents then said: 'When we tried to put our foot down, she said that we didn't love her and didn't care for her'. (Psychiatric Social Worker)

Typically, an attempt was made to overpower a vulnerable family. About a month later a placement was offered in order to 'take control out of their hands'. Jane's parents declined saying they would 'lose control' and Jane would 'have difficulty fitting in again' when she was discharged:

Mother wanted to cope – she felt that child guidance was getting nowhere. (Psychiatric Social Worker)

This raises alarm about practice standards. Rather than a continuing dialogue about differing perceptions of the situation, the assessor criticised Jane's mother's ambivalence, 'exhibiting a conflict of loving and rejecting feelings'. Such clashes of opinion and difficulty confronting conflict could be addressed through training programmes.

As frequently happened, the parents capitulated. Within two days of this interview, mother said that it was 'beyond her now to get her daughter up', and she did 'not know what to do'. Jane was a 'lot of bother' and 'beyond her control'. She was hitting Jane and 'sick of the whole family on her back.'

The lack of a mutual agreement that this was a situation concerning all the family, let alone wider society, was the main driver when cases collapsed:

The case lapsed through mother's default. (Mother) could not accept that Sally's stomach pains might have an emotional basis, and we were not able to help her gain much insight into her relationship with her daughter. (Psychiatrist)

The opening chorus – 'it's the child who has the problem' – became a refrain which allowed parents to abdicate their responsibilities:

> *Father did not attend, and mother said she did not approve of them coming, and wanted to opt out. Heather has been stealing again, and they had not undertaken any of our suggestions.*

DISPLACEMENT

The interviews were not considered faulty. Assessors shifted responsibility for failure to three locations:

- The family who did not wish to undertake therapy;
- The family members who could or would not make the prescribed changes;
- The child whose 'mentally disturbed' behaviour continued unabated.

Lack of cooperation produced an intractable situation, as exemplified in the process of treating Lisa's (fifteen) 'bouts of severe depression'.

> *Made progress initially, but we recognised it would take much longer to achieve any change in the family. We have not made as much progress as we would have liked because (adoptive mother) became quite paranoid about family work. (Adoptive father) struggled on in what little cooperation was left between ourselves and the family. (Psychiatrist)*

Responsibility for failure was heaped on mothers:

> *In a sense I think this is mother's way of informing us that she was covertly rejecting and had been for a long time. (Psychiatrist)*

The basis for all these suppositions could have been discussed in supervision.

CONFORMITY

Some families readily complied with worker's recommendations, but children sustained their challenging behaviour and accepted placements.

> *Heather was very happy with the idea. Saw it as constructive and not a punishment.*

Jane's family visited the adolescent unit and everyone agreed to admission:

> *Mother seemed to be most anxious about this course of action but was reassured by Jane.*

Five months from that point, Jane's cooperation continued, and she moved without protest to the hostel.

MINIMALISATION

Assessors regarded their technology as harmless, despite the concerns that should accompany the prospect of medication or a 'parentectomy' (Framrose, 1978):

> *The family situation is very bad and Heather is getting most of the rejection from father. She is much more depressed and cries a lot. I think it would be a great help if she came out of the family situation at least during part of the year. (Psychiatrist)*

In the absence of the client's perspective, it is all too easy to forget that treatments can be harmful. Any intervention that separates a child from family and friends is an extreme measure, which, in the view of the Children's Legal Centre (1991) should only be considered when a child or others are at risk of immediate or serious injury.

CONVICTEDNESS

> *It became abundantly clear that circumstances at home are going to prevent success in getting (Harriet 15.2) back to her comprehensive school. (Psychiatrist)*

This argument tapped into a primary objective of the service to ensure that the child is in education (Aldgate, 1991). (This was undoubtedly of enormous value to the long-term outlook for the children.) By inference it is also hiding the possibility that, in these cases, the CAMHT outpatient service could not alter home life.

URGENCY

Announcements about increased risk of harm. 'A crisis arose. Danger it will disrupt' (Angela) requires probing. Do crises demand removal from home, or another community-based crisis intervention technique? (Gutstein, 1988) Are there many crises in childcare work? Who is setting the thresholds for intervention? Does benign neglect have a place?

In summary, together with a considerable overload of cases and associated pressure on time, the following six factors either produced or hid technical inadequacy:

- irreconcilable viewpoints
- displacement
- conformity
- minimalisation
- convictedness
- urgency.

Resources

> *The hostel would appear to offer so many of the facilities which Sonia presently needs: a base for family work; the availability of individual therapy, well-established staff with good experience in dealing with children with emotional problems; the opportunity to live with her peer group; access to a choice of schools; and a home environment which affords creative activities out of school. (Guardian ad litem)*

Recognition of the powerful grip of resources upon the manufacture of assessments of need has driven recent changes in social policy (DH, 1989(b); NHS and Community Care Act, 1991). The empirical world demonstrates both their critical influence at decision-making points (Chapter IX), and how, even in small, self-sufficient agencies with limited options, this driver can be made inconspicuous. A small cluster of common arguments about need and efficacy readily justified the transformation to (more detrimental invasive) residential remedies (Barask, 1986; Utting, 1991):

PREVENTING DETERIORATION

She will relapse if returned home.

PREVENTING FAMILY BREAKDOWN

There is great family stress. Danger it will disrupt.

ACCESSING SPECIAL SERVICES

To assess the problem more fully, make a sensible plan for her future … Psychotherapy … Family group to be seen regularly to resolve some of their conflicts. (Psychiatrist regarding Samantha, hospital inpatient)

Social skills, independence training graded re-entry to school. (Psychiatrist regarding Lotte hospital day patient)

At first glance the 'set' of justifications contrasts with the reasons why social workers choose placement away from home, namely in response to family breakdown, to protect from abuse, and/or to control intolerable behaviour (Packman et al., 1986). Yet these factors were also present in many CAMHT cases. Obscuring the similarity between clients through the use of different language, maintains artificial distinctions between agencies. These were essentially the same clients. The only difference lay in the remedy. (For example an NHS or SSD bed). The empirical evidence lends powerful support to the unification of child welfare services in the same way that the health and social welfare needs of adults will be met by one organisation. (Primary Care Trust).

In addition to casework factors, resource-driven actions were underpinned by some more general features:

PRECEDENT

History and previous experience powerfully influence the choice of a resource. From the 1960s the hostel was part of the fabric of this particular child guidance service. It was opened in 1949 by a local education authority to care for maladjusted evacuee children:

Settled extremely well away from home. I would suggest transfer to the hostel so that Sonia can continue her schooling in peace and security. She will relapse if she goes home. It is undesirable for her to remain in hospital. She should be symptom free and does not need medication. I must continue to supervise her as she tends to retreat from stress by complaining of physical symptoms ... Given the kind of excellent management she can expect at the hostel, I think she will do well. (Psychiatrist)

Enthusiastic recommendations for the hostel were based on 'tradition' which 'does not have to concern itself with whether other systems are more true' (Witkin, 1995, p.84). Cultural practices are reinforced by satisfactory outcomes:

The reasons for which we admitted Sonia remain the same. She is quite an able girl, who given stable strong support, will achieve reasonable educational standards which will stand her in good stead for the future. (Psychiatrist)

Almost without exception, the young people immediately commenced regular school attendance and settled without protest into hostel life. Nichola wrote to her friend Carol Ann, who was still back, in the adolescent unit:

This place is really good. You'd love it! I've got to see Dr (X). We're going to discuss if I can 'cope here'. You've gotta come soon! Get on and get out of that dump. The (hostel) isn't bad (Sic).

Precedent grows from stereotypical activity. In the face of confusion and uncertainty, the restriction of choice gives the situation stability:

Left to herself, Sonia would not maintain regular attendance at school or get down to the work that is necessary for achievement. (Educational Psychologist)

Enthusiasm for the hostel was supported by the belief that it was not stigmatising. It was not 'care', nor a 'special' school, but was part of the education service. Nor was it obvious that it was a psychiatric resource. Occasionally the hostel acted as second best to the hospital when parents would not agree to that admission. Overall, parents and children found the service not dissimilar to a boarding school and very acceptable, particularly as there were no fees.

In contrast with social work practitioners who regard substitute care as a sign of failure (Short Report, 1984), the assessors were convinced about the additive value of their resources:

This hostel provides very considerable support to girls of her age (Ellie 14.10), with group therapy and input by an excellent staff. Hopefully she will stay until she completes her exams in two years. There is no hope of her returning to her comprehensive school because daily attendance is quite difficult for her to maintain. (Psychiatrist)

Similarly, the adolescent unit was seen as a 'warm growth-giving place', where children could 'flourish'. The few complaints were ignored. Nothing was allowed to impact on the legend of success.

I (teacher) have been conscious ever since I first saw Betty of a strong sense of unhappiness in being away from home and in having no positive prospect of a return there. I have every admiration for the hostel and the splendid work done there, but I have never felt that it was particularly suited to Betty's needs. I am aware of the turmoil which was present in the home before admission, but it, nevertheless, seemed to me that she has a place in her home despite her problems.

This was a direct challenge to the therapeutic strategy. The complainant continued:

I am disturbed by the fear that a prolonged absence from Betty's home could set up a form of resentment in her mind. She is near the end of her school career but ill equipped to face the move into the workaday world without the love and security of home to support her. Perhaps you could present this viewpoint to the conference.

This commentary concurs with a general observation, that very limited preparation for independent living was offered during placement. There is a danger in 'shared care' arrangements that neither parents nor carers will address this task. Betty was admitted to the hostel aged 13.9 and discharged by her mother aged 15.2. She was readmitted six months later at parent's request:

We see little alternative but to return her to you as you recommend it so strongly. We trust that you will be able to keep us informed this time of her progress so that we may work together to her advantage.

Betty stayed at the hostel for a further four months. (Analysis of the residential service concurred with this parent's view that, communication with carers was insufficient.)

PRIVATE OWNERSHIP

When access to medication, placements and so on is unobstructed, alternative options will rarely be considered. Not only did their accessibility enhance professional activity these solutions could be used for bargaining:

Both my (Psychiatrist) recommendation, and (Sonia's adoptive parents) agreement not to contest the application (for a care order) were firmly based on the hostel proposal.

GATEKEEPING

With parental agreement, transfer was only dependent on the availability of a bed. Although a local authority education officer acted as gatekeeper to the hostel, such powers had long since been usurped. A nominated Psychiatrist governed admissions, and merely sent courtesy letters to the titular head:

A bright girl about to start GCSEs. Ellie (14.10) has high aspirations and needs teaching in three languages.

Independent gatekeeping is essential (Taylor et al., 1980), for small agencies. Such intrusion introduces gravitas. The disjunctions and discomforts produced by raising key questions are crucial if escalation in the style of service delivery is to be a managed process. Is this the right course for the child and family? If treatment has failed, can another agency help? Have other childcare resources been disregarded? Can anyone in the family/friendship network offer help? What are the child's views? Is this the most cost-effective option? Who should have priority? And so on. Effective gatekeeping should extend the time that options are kept open, and can be a diversionary mechanism (Masson, 1992).

Summary

Evaluating the performance of an agency that did not have consistently applied thresholds has clearly demonstrated the influence of resources at decision-making points. Evidence has been presented that 'in-house' resources (medication, residential care and so on) are valuable assets in another way because their usage can hide incompetence and overwhelm rival agencies. Evaluation will threaten the stability of any agency that relies heavily on the ownership of a limited range of resources (Bateson, 1979). The empirical evidence contradicts Little's contention that: 'Children find themselves in specialised establishments ... because exceptional circumstances give rise to problems which cannot be met in any other way.' (Little and Kelly, 1996, p.196). What has been shown is that actors invest energy in creating fit with services and create text to convince others that this is the best, indeed only way, to meet the child's needs.

Residential care in the 1990s served a group of very challenging children, children about whom least is known, and, importantly, for whom previous interventions were inadequate. For some children (Bullock, 1992), residential care is the most appropriate placement, but the findings strongly suggest that careful reappraisal of performance and consideration of community-based alternatives should be triggered at precisely the point when all else is said to have failed. Then the group of children, for whom residential care will be the most effective outcome, can be selected by criteria based on their needs rather than those of professionals.

Minimal Intervention

A ground rule against which practice should be set is that all intervention is restricted, as far as is compatible with safety. Maintaining that position is extremely difficult, not least because of the judgmental nature of British society. The process of restricting intervention is like climbing a ladder. On the bottom rung are clients who would suffer greatly if left in the situation. They must be helped to climb upwards. In the absence of immediate danger, points of transition should be reframed as signals to stay on the same rung, in order to reappraise the quality of work to date. The first premise is that because social constructions are interpretations, they are available for reanalysis. Secondly, a principle of more of the same or 'parallel substitution' should prevail. 'Family sessions' had been the original treatment of choice for Gill, but her father 'refused to attend'. One 'parallel substitution' occurred, and Gill was seen weekly by a trainee clinical psychologist. Her mother met regularly with the Psychiatric Social Worker.

An auditor can draw attention to specific processes that militate against 'good enough' performance. Here, 'vertical substitution', that is a more invasive intervention, was efficiently justified by accentuating the problem. For Gill, after seven months, a Psychiatrist declared:

> *Various psychiatric treatments have been to no avail. There is no possibility of improving the mother-daughter relationship while she remains at home.*

Careful reflection upon the quality of service delivery up to this point, could prevent climbing away from the simplest interventions.

Although Judy has been going to school, she had shown hysterical symptoms and been grossly manipulative. She had a histrionic outburst in front of the school doctor who, with the parents' agreement, arranged immediate readmission. (Psychiatrist)

Such a draconian approach stops any difficulties persisting. It does not allow attempts at small changes and observation of the effects. Lone workers find it particularly difficult to manage high levels of risk.

There is a much larger dimension to minimalist practice. The context required to support it demands fundamental and far-reaching changes to the quality of the national environment for children (Hodgkin and Newell, 1996). Sticking with difficult and risky cases requires optimism, a belief in simplicity, and a sea of ordinary opportunities and resources with which to support healthy development.

As will be discussed in the conclusion, these must be part of the ingredients for a new child welfare service.

Reflective Practice

Decision making is reflexive (Steier, 1991), the presence of the social actor cannot be ignored. Is entering rescue mode an emotional response to situations? Distress is provoked by working with unpredictability (Menzies, 1970), high levels of expressed emotion, even fear of litigation. These dimensions to practice are heavily suppressed in medical environments. 'Holding' on to conflict and distress requires practitioners to pause rather than rush about. Assessors, as we have seen, rarely reviewed work in progress. For example, Nina (14.5) had been stealing and missing school for a term. The following areas for therapy had been identified:

Relationships with her peer group, and family …

Respite from the anxieties created by her mother's attention in her own right …

Counselling about her father's death, educational opportunity to promote her development. (Psychiatrist)

At the point when 'no efforts to date have succeeded in getting her back to school', the plan devised to address Nina's needs should have been reviewed. Instead, the child, alloyed to her distress, was quickly handed over to the hostel. Generally, there was only one chance with any type of therapy. The inadequacies of talk were neatly avoided by shifting the locus of failure from therapeutic effectiveness on to parental inadequacy (Chapter VII). Placement renewed optimism (Dingwall et al., 1983). It was an investment in the changes that the child could make on her own:

> *I hope that (Tara 14.7) will use her time at the hostel to sort out some of her feelings about herself and her family, as well as to concentrate on her school work. (Psychiatric Social Worker)*

A language must develop which positively connotes failure as a helpful sign. Fallibility must be brought into the public domain because learning from mistakes opens up new possibilities.

Conclusion

Evaluators can be confident of the productiveness of textual analysis as a method of performance analysis. Asking why? and how? what is gained? and what is lost by actions? Should not simply provoke new reductionist answers if difference and disagreement are valued as developmental tools in domains where there are few right answers. It may be that the method (of reading) is always slightly destructive in tenor. Experiments with its application in other domains will make this clearer, but I think it is largely because the 'reading' should only be one half of the equation. The other and more important half is the conversation that it provokes about practice effectiveness and efficiency. It has not been possible to ask what errors or misunderstandings this auditor has perpetrated.

Attention has been drawn to how professionals make judgments under conditions of uncertainty and deal with inadequacies in working practices. Their designs for change from one form of service delivery to another can signal the need for:

- Reappraisal of performance to date.
- Consideration of inadequacies.
- Open sharing of dilemmas.
- Pause for reflection.
- Broad consultation.
- Creative 'parallel substitutions', or more of the same.

This structured way of examining the quality of decision making suggests that generally CAMHTs should evaluate:

- The referral process.
- The assessment process.
- Management oversight, supervision and support to decision making.
- The quality of holistic work.
- The quality of inter and multidisciplinary communication.

The CAMHT was riddled with discounting processes that kept the curious at bay and the show on the road. Human service organisations need to attract reluctant traditionalists and lateral thinkers who have an enthusiasm for building a researching and learning culture (Whitaker and Archer, 1989). A social world that is unafraid to make things strange, pursues 'reasoned consensus rather than tradition (knowing that) it carries with it a notion of a judgement of adequacy' (Witkin, 1985, p.85), and the prospect of altered text.

The following two chapters describe the models of decision making derived from the qualitative analysis.

Chapter IX
A DECISION-MAKING MODEL

This chapter will show that to a significant extent, decisions are not related to the circumstances of individual service users, nor are they simply resource driven, but are heavily bound up with shortfalls in earlier interventions (Taylor, 2000). Decision making in human service organisations is a dynamic and interactive process (Robinson, 1987). Importantly, as will be shown, decisions are the predictable products of a cultural ensemble of contemporary, historical and socio-political factors.

A model for exploring the quality of critical decisions in real time was produced from the empirical data. It is especially applicable in agencies dominated by professional groups because it affords a way of exploring work that is predicated upon 'professional judgement' (Dowie and Elstein, 1988). It can be applied by practitioners, teams, managers and evaluators, and enriched by the presence of service users.

Decision-making Points

Decisions are as difficult to capture and explore as soap bubbles because of their 'transformative' nature (Berg, 1992). In identifying 'organised moments' (Chrishe, 1985) or 'case-turning points' (Bryer, 1988) they begin to appear to be the discrete products of professional analysis. In the empirical world they are signalled by clear-cut changes in service provision, for example, when a case is referred from one agency to another, or the focus of casework changed from work with the family to individual work, or from outpatient clinic to a residential placement:

Admit at once as the family appear at crisis point. (Psychiatrist)

Decisions can be pictured as layered spheres. Each layer acts like a chemical catalyst to speed up reactions without being altered itself.

A description of three such layers in the empirical world follows.

TERTIARY CATALYSTS

These form a dense core. The empirical universe contained some interdependent and powerful elements:

- A unified theory.
- The socio-political history of the agency.
- A coherent value system.

If any core factors were altered, an agency would be radically altered, or destroyed.

Theory and History as Catalysts

The CAMHT thrived on a theoretical approach to emotional disturbance that originated in the nineteenth century (Parry-Jones, 1984) and grew into an institutionally situated ideology. Workers focussed on children's emotions and behaviours and their relationship with their mothers (Zeitlin, 1986). This perspective was actively challenged from the mid-1970s (Barker, 1973; Totman, 1979), and child psychiatry was especially vilified (Hoghughi, 1977; Pearson, 1975). The empirical world (ninety-nine cases: 1977 to 1988) was a paradigm of that transitional period. Modern thinkers attributed children's behaviour to social interaction (Herbert, 1978), the environment, and the way the family as a system functioned (Hersov, 1986). A profound shift in the perception of children was under way (Peterson and Gill, 1986). Far from being impervious to the vagaries of the adults, some children were seen to be struggling in the face of family conflict (Coleman and Hendry, 1990) and reconstitution (Cockett and Tripp, 1994). For some practitioners, the family and not the 'identified patient' became the focus for their intervention (Bentovim et al., 1987). Others integrated family therapy with pre-existing psychodynamic approaches (Will and Wrate, 1985).

This CAMHT fluctuated between old and new ways:

> *The most effective treatment has lately proved to be family therapy. I am not entirely sure that (Sandra's 14.2) father could cope with this. An alternative is individual psychotherapy, and this I would like to arrange if we cannot achieve the ideal of family therapy. (Psychiatrist)*

During the decade, challenges to the hegemony of psychiatry were evident in an oft-recycled debate over the name of the agency. The title of the service was changed (in the early 1980s) from 'Child Guidance Clinic' to 'Child, Family and Adolescent Psychiatric Service'. This signified the continuing dominance of psychiatry, but at the same time differentiated the clinic from competitors. (Nearby a 'family therapy unit', had been established by social workers and psychologists.) Later there were proposals for neutral titles: 'The Blenheim Clinic', 'The Child and Family Service', and the 'Family Consultancy'. Whether the psychiatric component should be hidden by such titles, is a moot point. The launch in 1989 of 'The Child and Adolescent Mental Health Team' showed that the original values and beliefs remained. This limited enquiry into the tertiary catalysts has exposed the political facets and fragility of the theoretical base.

Agency Preservation

> Power is about the politics of everyday life.
>
> Clegg, 1989, p.149

Organisations have a vested interest in survival. Self-sufficiency, detachment and isolation support elitism. Adjusting 'problems' and 'risks' into manageable shapes is a particularly powerful preservative of social worlds. The combination of tertiary catalysts produced a bounded and particular, medico-socio-educational 'space' (Parton, 1991) in which 'to qualify, to classify, to differentiate, and to judge' (Foucault, 1977, p.184) a world of children. Underlying this observation lay a major analytical theme. Beyond their specialist language and reserved resources very little differentiated this child welfare agency from others in the arena.

> Adherence to organisational policies and practices is always an
> integral part of problem solving or decision making.
>
> Cicourel, 1987, p.54

Strategies for the maintenance of boundaries will be found where
several agencies are competing for work. Here both internal and
external actors subscribed to the secrecy and etiquette used to
maintain this special place. Universal consensus and conformity
defined the territory into which children and families were absorbed.

SECONDARY CATALYSTS

These elements have middle-ranking influence on 'the decision-
making point'. In the empirical world they were:

- The questionable quality of previous interventions.
- The continuing challenging behaviour of clients.

Budgetary constraints, or caseload weighting devices, were not
drivers in the empirical world, but are likely to be located either
here or in the 'primary' category (see later) in other agencies.

Technical Failure

An inadequate professional performance speeds up catalysis and
was found at all points of transition from referral onwards. It was
mostly hidden, and, importantly, unrecognised.

> *How this situation has arisen I find difficult to establish, but I think
> that it may have to do with problems the parents have in their own
> relationship. (Psychiatrist)*

The very presence of a readily available rescue remedy, inevitably
makes it hard to sustain family work, when the going is tough and
the outcome unpredictable. The arguments generated at these
times, that 'nothing else can be done' in such 'hopeless' situations,
are designed to justify pulling out. The consequence for the
children was that of the total cohort, forty-eight per cent moved
directly to the hostel. Of the remainder, fifty-two per cent were
admitted to the Adolescent Psychiatric Unit before moving to the
hostel. Four per cent of the total cohort was recycled through the
hostel to the hospital.

Client Distress

A turning point was provoked when the child's behaviour was unchanged. Situations were described as too 'dangerous' to continue working, whilst the child remained at home:

> *I think she (Caroline) may already have been exposed to quite severe punishment, and there is a danger in a situation like this of cruelty. (Psychiatrist)*

PRIMARY CATALYSTS

The part that these play in decision making cannot be overemphasised. They strongly influence the 'locally situated routines' in organisations (Berg, 1992). In the empirical world they were:

- The social construction.
- The resources.

Other social worlds may use descriptions of client 'need' as their primary catalyst, but this will conceal other drivers, particularly resource availability or economic constraints.

The Social Construction

The social construction was the most distinctive catalyst (Chapter IV). The shift from work which involved both child and parent(s), to work focussing on the child alone, was strongly influenced by a formulation which offered 'escape clauses', to justify different service provision.

Resources

The malleability of the 'diagnosis' was strongly supported by easily accessible remedies. The removal of a distressed child from the family and into a residential setting, was justified by all the other catalysts and achieved by this one. These 'routine remedies' provided a stable background 'in which human activity may proceed with the minimum of decision making most of the time' (Berger and Luckman, 1966, p.71). However, contrary to their view that 'a background of habitualised activity opens up a foreground of deliberation and innovation' (ibid.), such creativity was not detectable. It was submerged by habitual patterns of conduct, a welter of other catalysts, and drowned by off the shelf remedies.

Routines sustain 'the normal everyday state of affairs' (Giller and Morris, 1981, p.54). Professional responses to the 'delinquent' children studied by these authors (ibid.), were, like the CAMHT, regularised because the practitioners had access to a solution.

THE COMBINED EFFECT OF THE CATALYSTS

Catalysts produce order. Risk management strategies (Gutstein et al., 1988; Packman et al., 1986; Stainton Rogers and Stainton Rogers, 1989) are mandated by expectations that challenging behaviour will be brought within acceptable norms (or cured) by welfare agents. Vernon and Fruin (1986) concluded that Social Workers responded by arranging placements. The process is more dynamic than they argued. Unpredictability and certainty coexist but have varying levels of influence throughout the life of a case. Social work responses to situations that are 'seriously menacing or suspenseful' (Rojek et al., 1988, p.116) are based 'not on the poverty and disruption of children's lives as such, but on the risks and difficulties in relationships and behaviours which stem from such circumstances' (Packman, 1989, p.87). The same drivers applied to the CAMHT, despite their emphasis on the psychological damage that attended risky and chaotic situations (Rose, 1990).

> *(Lindsay) is showing signs of disturbance, and I would be very concerned if we did not intervene at this stage. (Psychiatrist)*

The secondary catalysts (the sustained distress of the child, and the inadequacy of attempts to produce change) (Rizzo, 1993) were managed by:

- the tertiary catalysts;
- the primary catalyst of the social construction which offered many options for intervention; and
- the routine remedies ranging from surveillance to asylum.

It is easy to underestimate just how provocative these situations are, even to trained and experienced people who have the additional support of team membership (Chapter X; Woodhouse and Pengelly, 1991). The children were distressed, angry, rejected, and profoundly unhappy. Samantha became 'hysterical' at school. At home she was 'cutting her arms with a razor blade, and burning herself with cigarettes'. It is very saddening to think of young people being so troubled, and some of the texts transmitted the worker's sense of hopelessness. So they drew on the combined effect of the tertiary and primary catalysts to convert the unpredictable (Bosk, 1988) into a 'new certainty' (Howe, 1994). Perhaps even the acts of writing records can anaesthetise anxiety, as the author 'donates meaning' to the situation.

> 'Assessments' and 'diagnostic formulations' were riddled with the 'uncertainty (which) creeps into medical practice through every pore.'
>
> Eddy, 1988, p.45

Decision making under conditions of uncertainty is observable 'with endless regularity in medical settings' (Cicourel, 1987, p.347) and throughout human welfare organisations. Any agency that offers to manage risk is rewarded by a gain in power, but the evidence suggests that their coping mechanisms may exact an inappropriately high price from the consumer (Mattinson and Sinclair, 1979; Taylor, 2000). They may be subjected to unnecessary or over-intrusive intervention designed to protect the assessor from the condition of 'not knowing'. (Litigation is another growing driver). Chapter VIII proposed that not knowing and not acting busy should be encouraged. It is an honest reflection of much of the state of the art in child welfare, and offers opportunity for more 'needs-led' outcomes to prevail.

Practical Application

The 'sphere' can be applied to single cases by practitioners and interagency teams (Chapter X), as well as by managers charged with setting general quality standards for agencies. As an example, Blagg and Yule (1984) reported on a social world that had three treatment styles (for comparable groups of school phobic children aged eleven to sixteen years). These were:

- Rapid behavioural treatment with the child at home.
- Admission to a hospital unit.
- Home tuition and outpatient psychotherapy.

When they looked at how children came to be in hospital, they concluded that the process was:

> An outcome of patterns of referral, and the restrictions and bias of the professionals involved, rather than a careful considered intervention weighed against alternative community approaches, and the outcomes are no better.

Ibid., p.12

Combining this model for deconstructing crucial decisions, with the method of reading (introduced in Chapter I), will reveal the detail of the 'restrictions and bias' that are influencing practice. This style of performance assessment will explore:

- The position of the agency amongst others.
- The history, and origin of the agency. Does it survive in one place and not another?
- The theoretical basis from which it acts, and the competing perspectives.
- The effectiveness of interventions.
- The quality of relations with extramural agencies.
- The relations of ruling within the agency.
- The recognition of and response to poor performance.
- The quality of work with carers and clients.
- The nature of the social construction.
- The mechanisms which permit or prohibit more intrusive interventions.

Conclusion

The concept of a sphere containing layers of catalysts which play into decisions, offers a way of unpacking and weighing decisions. For example, in a matter before the court, the opinion of an expert commissioned by the parents may be a primary catalyst, and the social worker with a perspective on the day-to-day life of a child is likely to be relegated to an outside position. If a debate ensued about whether the needs of the child are being put first it could be that these drivers would be reversed. Decisions in the empirical world were strongly influenced by:

TERTIARY CATALYSTS

Subterranean features and strategies which ensure that the organisation persists.

SECONDARY CATALYSTS

Which introduce or maintain a demand to create change.

PRIMARY CATALYSTS

Agency components and tactics which generate and govern the business.

It has been shown that decisions are the occasioned products of their worlds. They are catalysed by a group of factors, some of which can be identified by textual analysis. Most factors suggested by the ethnography are likely to be found more generally in welfare organisations, but their influence may differ. Their identification should make evaluation of the quality of performance available for external influence. This is particularly useful for those 'well-placed persons' (Goffman, 1983) who can intrude in agencies where it is claimed that decisions are predicated upon specialist knowledge and judgment which cannot be located and analysed by the uninitiated. Two ethnographic themes have been united. Firstly, the very strong norms against unpredictability and against admitting that the technology is primitive. Secondly, the complex rituals and practices which are instrumental in risk management and in obscuring technical failure. Acknowledging the effects of these factors could transform the way business is transacted. If this results, as it should, in sticking with a child rather than transferring the work to others, then the toll on the practitioner may be too great. Groups can tolerate complexity and ambiguity more than individuals.

The next chapter draws on the ethnography to explore ways of keeping vulnerable and challenging children within their environments.

Chapter X

THE EMBRACE OF POWER

Lindsay's (14.10) disturbance is the result of going to school from a house full of tension and stress. I have tried to work with the family to overcome some of this, but having seen them all together with the severely ill father, it is plain that no girl can be expected to survive without showing some difficulties in this household. I am therefore recommending that it would be in her best interests if she had a hostel place. (Psychiatrist)

This chapter will describe four models of interdisciplinary working seen in the data and present a design for improvement.

The CAMHT sat at one extreme of a continuum of agency types. It was an autonomous, unaccountable 'professional bureaucracy' (Mintzberg, 1989) which had collared a particular market and was buffered from cultural change. A special language and particular interventions produced a neat, stable and cohesive system. Towards the other end of this continuum are eclectic pluralistic organisations with elaborate systems of accountability. These are more malleable and open to influence by the consumer's world. (Locality-based Social Services teams sit slightly to the right of a midpoint.) Studying an extreme agency illuminates the middle ground.

This first section describes the dominant model of interaction, and communication, exhibited by the CAMHT. Its features and some of the ways that it sustained itself were striking.

A 'Closed-complex' Model

> It is just as naïve for theorists of social regulation to assume that such systems (of child protection) do and can work functionally together as it is for central government guidance.
>
> Parton, 1991, p.207

Figure X.1   *A 'closed-complex' system*

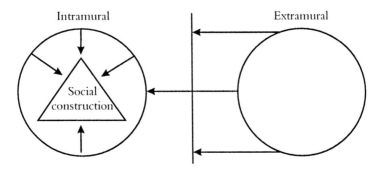

Intramural   Extramural

Social construction

Arrows represent the movement of information. Some extramural information was absorbed, but most was generated internally, and very little was released to outsiders. The flow was constrained by the rules and rituals that have been described earlier.

STRUCTURE AND INTERACTION

The CAMHT claimed that a permanent 'multidisciplinary' team was an efficient way to produce holistic assessments and deliver services. However, as has been shown, there were shortfalls in performance quality. In these teams, 'mutual trust' and 'confidence' was highly valued. Confidence in each other was important given the abundance of judgement and guesswork in their work. This form of 'knowing' each other also acted as an 'agency preservative' because it quelled rivalry between professional groups.

To maintain a steady state, newcomers from any profession, Social Workers in particular, were initially deskilled. Early induction into the rules of conduct and procedure, and the formulae for case types (Marsh, 1990) converted them into community members (Paley, 1987). Bateson (1979) described the repeated activity of seeking other examples of some event to confirm a story and the rules about it as 'abduction'. 'The whole of art, the whole of science are instances or aggregates of instances of abduction, within the human sphere.' (ibid., p.157) Inculcation with the legends about children weakened the incomer's potential to destabilise the system. Abduction was the primary way in which the legends grew and incomers worked their passage. Repetition scaffolded the system:

> The converse of this statement is that change will require various sorts of relaxation or contradiction within a system of presuppositions.
>
> Ibid.

Any contradiction would weaken a system designed, in large part, to manage situations that were construed as highly dangerous. Hence, tertiary catalysts, including a script which echoed the legends and made the stories very robust (Hall, 1991), was very resistant to change. A healthy multidisciplinary system will value the imported skills of newcomers.

Strategies For System Maintenance

In a context of impoverished interagency communication, the possession of an armoury of problem-solving devices maintained the 'closed-complex' system. Limited communication supported the impression that a magical cure lay within the agency.

> *Better left to us at the clinic because I think this will be a rather intensive business which will require careful monitoring. (Psychiatrist to General Practitioner)*

The views and services of other agencies were lost at this point. For example, Education and Social Services saw Sonia as:

> *An attractive girl who was mature socially and intellectually, but emotionally very confused and unhappy.*

Jointly these agencies proposed that Sonia:

> *Remain in as stable situation as possible (In the SSD observation and assessment unit) until the problems and issues can be probed further (and) for however long it takes for her situation to be examined. It would be beneficial if her schooling could be maintained, so that she does not have too many changes all at once in her life.*

This representative case illustrates how professional disharmony exposed children to multiple assessments and moves. Shifts in control of the case diagram (Appendix II) were driven by several catalysts:

- bids by a professional to gain case control;
- ineffective practice;
- the continued distress of the child;
- the exclusion of actors. (In Sonia's case, two powerful actors: the court and psychiatry, colluded in order to remove subordinates.)

Poor communication and collaboration is hidden in 'closed-complex' systems. It would be exposed if referrers were interested in outcomes:

> *Because of this complex picture (of Sonia), there has been considerable difficulty in deciding on the most appropriate plan. (Psychiatrist)*

The 'difficulty' arose because extramural information and resources were ignored, not entirely because the case was complex. The complaints from excluded professionals deserved investigation:

> *I (General Practitioner) am interested to know how this case (Karen 8.11) has snowballed. I asked for a domiciliary (home visit from a Psychiatrist) some months back and was told that the case was in the hands of the Psychologist with your (Psychiatrist's) agreement. Could you ensure that all correspondence is circularised to keep manipulation to a minimum?*

The grudging communication of the CAMHT provoked ire at a regional secure unit (Millham et al., 1987):

> *General details were forwarded but no further information has been forthcoming e.g. developmental milestones – normal or not? Evaluation of current and previous family dynamics. Whereabouts of natural father – alive still? Origin and explanation for Michelle's (14.9) entrenched anti-authoritarianism reference, especially early teens?*

This insularity had serious consequences for Michelle:

> *These omissions leave a total assessment picture that is somewhat speculative and incomplete. We can evaluate her disposition and bearing within the unit quite fully, but it is not possible to relate this behaviour either to previous development, or to current family circumstances, nor to identify longer-term psychological patterns.*

A holistic picture might have countered the problematisation of the child:

> *She is challenging, confused and unhappy. Her future depends on her ability to dissipate her resentment and suspicion of all adults. (Secure Unit Manager)*

ACCOUNTING PRACTICES

Tracking the activity of workers provides a way of understanding the meaning of 'multidisciplinary' in a particular system. One of the most informative themes of the ethnography has been how a singular social construction can be produced, irrespective of whether one or several disciplines were involved. Despite, or because of, the tightly hierarchical structure, roles and tasks became blurred as people worked in different dyads and triads. This diffusion was least evident at times when psychiatrists assumed all the roles, which was an unsubtle exhibition of dominance and most evident when 'family therapy' was practiced. (Currently Community Psychiatric Nurses are mimicking autonomous behaviour in child and adult community mental health teams). Either way, there were no discernable differences between the practitioners, due to mutual subscription to a set of practices which did not belong exclusively to any specific discipline. Conjoint 'family therapy' acted as a form of 'riot control' because subordinate workers could be prideful in their work whilst settling for psychiatric hegemony.

Combining information of 'different sorts, or from different sources, results in something more than addition' (Bateson, 1979, p.78). This 'momentary gleam of enlightenment' (ibid., p.99), is like the way using two eyes gives depth to an image: the result is both different and unexpected. Combining different accounts, the 'multidisciplinary effect' could be expected to produce a whole greater than the sum of the parts, but in this closed-complex system there was insufficient space for such serendipitous and 'meta' accounts. Holistic pictures were lost, as overcomplicated narrowly focussed accounts eroded other perspectives in the process of 'subtraction and solidification' described in Chapter IV.

Claims that a particular organisational arrangement produces holistic assessments can be tested, not only by tracking information flow, but also by looking for 'added value' in the output. A disconnected assembly of different accounts would be inadequate.

DEVICES TO SAVE 'SOCIAL ENERGY'

Closed-complex systems are self-sustaining and conserve 'social energy'. This was a system in perpetual and predictable motion sustained by referrers who were political soulmates and intramural social actors who could be taken for granted.

This ivory tower was so inaccessible that many outsiders declined to send referrals because they would lose contact with the child. Maintaining fruitful relationships with external players requires considerable effort and commitment. For this team it was risky, because strangers might be inquisitive. Consequently, 'outsiders' were rarely given the opportunity to learn about the style of working and the valuable understanding of young people that was held by some within the clinic (NHS/HAS, 1995). By accepting that the doors were closed, the extramural players cooperated in the maintenance of the intramural world.

Three smaller scale models of interaction were formulated from the empirical evidence.

'Miniature Closed-complex' Systems

When tracking 'information transfer', and evaluating decision-making points, 'status', 'trust', and 'sabotaging strategies' could be seen to influence when, and with whom, communication occurred. These factors will diminish effective interaction and, in any agency system, could produce several miniature versions of 'closed-complex' systems. The links between psychiatry, the court, and to an extent Sonia's parents, were such a subsystem.

Figure X.2 *A miniature closed-complex system*

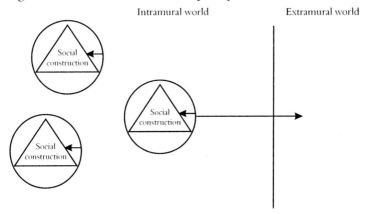

This is a fragmented and uncoordinated arrangement, ostensibly a multidisciplinary team, but the actors work in isolation. The closed-complex system has degraded. Several systems have formed, each chasing and affirming a specific and different story (represented by a triangle). Arguably, and certainly in some cases in the empirical world, this was the dominant model. Either each social actor was a quasi-psychiatrist or the voice of all but the psychiatric actor was erased. This can be a very efficient system and is not uncommon in medical settings.

There were faint traces of another model of interfacing with other agencies.

An 'Open-naïve' Model

Figure X.3 *An open-naïve system*

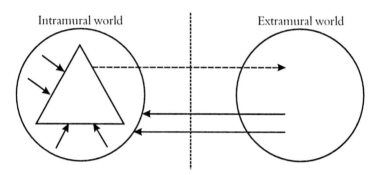

This primitive form of interagency collaboration was characterised by limited forays across a semi-permeable boundary. The information drawn from and fed back to the extramural world remained too limited to inform assessment and care planning effectively, and key players were excluded.

In the case of Sonia, the Community Social Worker struggled to exercise the legally binding duties of 'administrative parent' (Adcock et al., 1983):

Following recent events, I (Community Social Worker) think it is necessary to establish guidelines and put in writing future plans. These will be sent to everyone to prevent misunderstandings.

It is important that the relationship between Sonia and her natural mother should be allowed to develop slowly.

Ultimately, Social Services concluded that Sonia should live with her natural family, which drew this response from a Psychiatrist:

I hope there has been some misunderstanding because it was quite clear in everyone's minds that Sonia would remain at the hostel during term time until she had completed her examinations.

Stronger arguments were marshalled in an attempt to retain case control. Firstly, about the long-term outlook:

It is the concern of the multidisciplinary team who take responsibility for the programmes of care of the young people, that it would be a grave error to remove her at this stage and the prognosis for her continued good adjustment would be poor. We, therefore, strongly advise that the girl should remain at the hostel as planned on both education and treatment grounds. (Psychiatrist)

Secondly, about deprivation of specialist services:

The change in her attitude and stability since she has been at the hostel is quite dramatic and quite against the evidence of her previous behaviour. She has shown that she can accept reasonable control. She has also been able to make use of the group therapy process and is just beginning to improve her social skills in relationships with peers and authority. (Psychiatrist)

The psychiatrist did not attend a Social Services' 'review meeting' 'due to a prior commitment'. The head of the hostel attended:

As Sonia is in the care of the local authority, and they have the right to remove her from the hostel at any time, I felt I could only be as supportive to Sonia as possible. (Hostel manager)

Further protestations by the Psychiatrist drew a sarcastic response from the Social Services' manager:

Thank you so much for your letter. We were so very sorry that you were unable to be at the review where Sonia's future was discussed, as it would have been helpful to have your views at the time. (Social Services Team Manager)

The chance to consider the costs and benefits of the plan was lost:

Nevertheless, we must go ahead with our plan to rehabilitate Sonia

> *to what we now consider her home base, in the spirit of Tradmore County Council's policy towards children who are in our care. (Social Services Team Manager)*

Sonia's adoptive father tried to undermine this plan by asking the Psychiatrist if the proposal was 'a good idea', which drew the reply:

> *Afraid he cannot comment on the arrangements made by the Social Workers, as they did not ask his opinion. (Psychiatrist)*

Not strictly true. Still less supportive of the outside agency. Commenting on the child's best interests was, it appears, less important than struggling for power. In the absence of interdisciplinary collaboration, 'open-naïve' models are in some senses worse than 'closed-complex' ones, where, at least, the rules of the game are clear.

Summary

Ostensibly, the CAMHT was a miniature model of a mature, unfragmented social welfare service, which provided a holistic approach to children and families. Importantly, the ethnography illustrates the potential of such systems to 'coalesce' and lose different perspectives to transform from a multidisciplinary to a 'unidisciplinary' team.

'Closed-complex' models of organisation can be uncovered despite their processes and products appearing difficult to unravel. Questions can be raised about why they exist and in the form they take. Aspects of performance assessment include communication networks, the sequence of collaborative endeavours, and system maintenance strategies.

All three systems suppressed voices, made many skills redundant, and ultimately produced a significantly reduced picture of a child's world. Describing their 'frameworks' of power (Clegg, 1989) could be a way of provoking change.

New Directions in Working Together

In professional organisations, 'the one place in the world where you can act as if you were self-employed yet regularly receive a pay check', (Mintzberg, 1989, p.173), alterations to processes of interaction are generally evolutionary and very slow. This is particularly so if bureaucratic mechanisms are the change agents, and significant actors are maverick and generally non-compliant. Recent developments in interdisciplinary working practices (DH, 1988) have required central government enforcement to overcome the resistances (Frost et al., 1991) to alterations in relations of power (Parton, 1991). For example, the Secretary of State designed a framework of 'interagency case conferences', 'reviews' and 'core group' meetings for the management of child protection work (Home Office, 1991). These meetings enjoin anyone who has information to give or a need to gain it, to meet the family and other carers. These groups discuss changes and improvements. The next section explores the advantages of extending this idea further to:

- all children 'in need' as well as 'subject to harm';
- other client groups; and
- communities of need.

Combining the information from the ethnography with experience of the practices that are developing in interagency child protection work, produced germinal ideas for an 'open-complex' interdisciplinary model.

AN 'OPEN-COMPLEX' MODEL

The figure overleaf illustrates the overlapping of boundaries between several interdisciplinary subsets. Such open, non-habitualised and flexible forms of interaction will produce multifaceted accounts to drive decisions.

Figure X.4   *An 'open-complex' system*

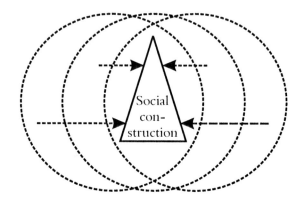

Individual Cases

The 'open-complex' system of interaction has a novel configuration of workers for each case. Delegates meet to discuss situations, pool and analyse information, and produce plans. These 'congresses' will be 'markers' permeating the process of each case and significant catalysts to decision making. Their tasks are to:

- Facilitate the exchange of information.
- Identify shortfalls in information.
- Produce a prioritised list of needs.
- Acknowledge differing views.
- Apply a rule of least detrimental intervention.
- Draw on egalitarian principles.
- Listen to the consumer's view.
- Retain different perspectives.
- Avoid predetermined outcomes.
- Apply research evidence.
- Identify any wider community of need.

The picture should be balanced and not entirely problem focussed, with the strengths in the system also made obvious. Professionals, managers, technicians and consumers gain both from improved communication and the cross-fertilisation of ideas, and from exposure of the myth that only certain actors have answers.

Community Development

Shortfalls at political and corporate management levels are, inevitably, played out within individual cases. Casework and community work (Payne, 1995) can be recombined if planners and contractors participate in meetings with clients. Congress is a creative way to communicate unmet needs and ideas for prevention directly to strategic development groups and politicians. Contact with 'real' service users will have considerable impact. It is an effective form of advocacy. Whilst the social energy of a system is conserved for the client and their world. In turn, the user voice will be appreciably less tokenistic. Single cases will draw attention to 'communities of need'. The resultant development of preventative services will divert potential clients into self-directed support service (DH, 1995(b)), and so reduce demand.

This recombination could affect an enormous number of consumers and create a world of meetings. Even with the application of new technology, (like videoconferencing), it does not progress interdisciplinary working practices far. However, it represents the notion of a sustained and multivocal conversation with people in difficulty, and the creation of an energised interface between individual and community needs. Creating and sustaining this style of conversation is a crucial and fundamental practitioner skill.

Moral and Political Aspects of Working Together

Congresses have the potential to be power-sharing cultures. Rather than power being gained and retained by common practice, or tyranny, it will move through the group, depending upon the skills and responsibilities that are required. So, the unqualified family support worker/aide would have case control when the primary tasks concern poverty or parenting practices. Valuing each way of understanding the situation will be a challenging aspect of practice, and most likely to be achieved through the trust that is developed by regular encounters.

The empirical findings support a 'value-based approach' that maintains 'openness (to the) uniqueness of each child and shared decision making' in order to produce 'normalised outcomes' (Welby, 1992, p.15). It will need to avoid the growth of a non-confrontative norm (Chapter III) in order to deal with conflict (Corby, 1987). A democratic ethic allows 'people to influence social choices that affect their lives' (Jordan, 1990, p.147), and choose 'offers (of) relevant and effective help and support' (ibid., p.165). So, congress must adopt a:

> Legitimate moral position – one of knowledge of the client's situation, and sharing his or her concerns, rather than one of superiority.
>
> Ibid.

The case-conferencing process in child protection (DH, 1988) has introduced people to the skills, benefits and challenges of collaborating (Hallet and Birchall, 1992) with families. Making this practice commonplace in social welfare, and exposing hidden and not so hidden agendas will create tension. This can be used positively to make difficult choices and achieve changes. This study has illustrated that the services provided reflect the limitations of the state of the art, as much as the restrictions imposed by resource constraints. It has shown that situations are simplified in order to manage complexity, and delete the contradictory factors which magnify ambiguity. Couple this with an axiom that there are few right answers in child welfare and the participants will be uncomfortable. Importantly this is the state most likely to give the client sonority.

> The notion of the perfect whole, the ultimate solution, in which all good things coexist, seems to me to be not merely unattainable but conceptually incoherent. We are doomed to choose, and every choice may entail an inseparable loss.
>
> Sir Isaiah Berlin
> *Guardian*, 7 November 1997, p.20

At some point choice has to be made about how, if at all, to help people in distress. A world of endless conversation might be considered a poor way to try to diminish people's troubles. They are, however, well-grounded ideas.

Leadership

There is a pivotal role for leaders (Lewis, 1994). They make 'case-turning points' transparent, and help groups to debate the issues (Janis, 1989). A keen acquaintance with the range of skills and services available, coupled with vision and creativity in sufficient measure to facilitate lateral thinking will be vital. (Thought-shower exercises might produce 'innovative' solutions.)

Groups will agree which catalysts are dominant and evaluate the quality of past interventions. Questions can be raised to ascertain what needs are being addressed, whether current best practice is being applied, and whether doing nothing is an option. Gradually this way of practice will become commonplace, and the leader will merely provide an independent opinion and turn up the volume for weak voices. As an agent of quality control in the system, the leader will measure effectiveness by:

- Tracking information transfer pathways.
- Monitoring case control trajectories.
- Identifying endpoints.
- Looking for subtraction and solidification.
- Assaying drift into closed-complex systems.

Helping groups to focus on the client's strengths rather than weaknesses demands a capacity to tolerate unpredictability and increased levels of risk. These 'guardians of the decision-making sphere' need to be keenly aware that systems have a potential to drift into a closed-complex state. In summary, leaders would be tasked to:

- Protect the value base.
- Ensure the groups are multi-vocal, and the client's voice is loud.
- Act as an advocate for dissenting views.
- Monitor the position of the alternative constructions.

- Announce drift to singular accounts and recipes.
- Track the locus of case control.

MEASURING INTERACTIONAL PATTERNS

The evidence suggests that if 'open and complex' systems are to produce assessments driven more extensively and rigorously by 'need' and not available resources, then measuring the pathway of information transfer on which they depend will be an influential device:

- Which actors provided information?
- Who is working with whom?
- Is some expertise missing?

Cross-boundary alliances should be evident in the replies. Mapping communication sequences may expose gaps that, if filled, could significantly affect interventions. Alternatively, it may confirm that the assessments, and recommendations for services are well founded.

MONITORING THE LOCUS OF CASE CONTROL

As an 'antihomeostatic device' (Bentovim et al., 1987), congress leaders guard against moves that produce equilibrium at the client's expense. It has been shown how readily case control can be gained in an unplanned and uncontrolled manner, and from the basis of very limited assessment. Applying the concept of a 'locus of case control' will identify:

- What actor has case control?

Any case transfer will be by mutual agreement:

> Varying approaches, tasks, and values in ways that enable each profession to fulfil its own job properly, and at the same time allows them to respect each other and to work together effectively.
>
> Stainton Rogers, 1989, p.11

Bearing in mind that poor interagency communication and lack of clarity about where responsibility rests has been at the heart of many child abuse tragedies (Butler Sloss, 1988; Reder et al.,

1993), coalescence might be counteracted by 'separating devices'. Skills held by only one discipline must be agreed by the group. Skills held by a number of disciplines can be utilised according to predetermined protocols, for example, cost effectiveness. Shared record keeping, could reflect and guide the process. For example, by showing where work is being duplicated.

It has been argued that even within 'closed' systems, other ways of construing the child's situation can be detected. To counter the suppression of these options the views of each agency and family must be heard without reference or deference to others. Repetition of these enquiries at case-turning points should counter the tendency for an initial assessment to reign unchallenged throughout the life of the case (Munroe, 1996). It is difficult to focus on bullying in the face of a more influential voice about 'anorexia'. The point is that the ascendant construction should be one arrived at by interagency agreement, on the basis of full information, and not by practices which oppress voices.

The degree to which healthy difference and creative tension is present can be explored by asking the interagency group:

- What do you remain puzzled about?
- What does not fit with the prevailing account?
- Who does not agree with the dominant assessment?

It may be impossible to make a new sense of things at the time of asking. The questions need to be repeated from time to time, with reminders about what remained perplexing. The aim is to establish an evidence-driven culture in which it is acceptable not to know and to resist the pressure to apply any solution. This will be difficult in the presence of carers and when interdisciplinary groups are still learning to be honest, let alone uninhibited. (Interestingly since 1999 this activity now occurs between expert witnesses in the legal arena.)

'Holding'

The evidence that few children subject to interdisciplinary child protection practices are separated from their family (DH, 1995), lay behind consideration of how to avoid applying drastic remedies. Groups can tolerate higher levels of risk (Woodhouse and Pengelly, 1991) and therefore have a capacity to 'hold on' to existing situations. Therefore congresses will retard the tendency to move into 'problem-solving mode'. If the focus is on 'relations' (Bateson, 1973), rather than the 'peculiarities of individuals' (Shotter and Gergen, 1989), uncertainty, back covering, scapegoating and conflicting dogma will undermine it.

Connecting Values to a New Theory

Values and theoretical constructs are inextricable. Though generally unspoken, they play into group attitudes about:

- What any person of this age and stage needs.
- What this particular person's world is like.
- The carers' effect on the person's behaviour.
- Who is meeting needs?
- The shortfalls, problems, concerns, risk.
- What must change?
- What is negotiable?
- Cooperativeness and partnership.
- Who can assist with achieving change?
- Whether non-intervention is an option.

A unified framework of statements which make theory, evidence and values explicit, represents a major task for the future. Could agreement be reached that children may communicate through behaviour only, that behaviour is a product of social interaction (Potter and Wetherall, 1987), not just a product of physiological or psychological processes, that the behaviour of carers affects children's behaviour as does their environment? A new, 'unified theory about children' could be built from scratch, from grounded, contemporary evidence. It would be a dynamic theory if constructed and reconstructed by conversation in virtual reality.

Conclusion

These ideas are an attempt to ensure that practice is innovative. Simple models of multidisciplinary and interagency interaction have been produced. Gradations of 'open' and 'closed' systems exist currently, and it cannot be assumed that legislation has impacted on them all.

Congress is a way of constantly rearranging interagency landscapes to produce dynamic frameworks of power. Integration of the decision sphere into this model offers a way of approximating more closely to a 'needs-led' service, and firmly integrating the consumer's voice amongst a range of disciplines. This chorus might compose new harmonies. The responsibility for identifying the needs of particular communities would be located alongside work with individuals and their families. Managers can integrate performance appraisal and strategic development by working amongst the consumers. This could lead to cross fertilisation, even the generation of commonality of need between previously apparently separate groupings.

The coherence of many of the themes produced by the ethnography enhanced a growing conviction that we need to develop a conversational and reflective social welfare milieu which will keep children safe without destroying their world.

Chapter XI
CONCLUSION

A thorough appraisal of the quality of professional and specialist work has proved possible even without direct individual appraisal and the observation of the team at work. Documents and records have revealed the formulae for action and the quality of interaction within a team and in relation to outsiders. It bears repeating that this was a specific audit of the service provided to ninety-nine out of approximately three thousand children over a period of ten years. This group (all girls) was selected because they were removed from the full-time care of their parent(s). This work was the most resource hungry and had the highest impact on service users.

The fine-grained analysis proved extremely fruitful. It unearthed a fascinating, if irreverent, history of a particular social world. Concepts such as 'case turning', 'social energy', and 'binary construction' can be tested for robustness and utility in different welfare fields. It has been shown that decisions are not predicated solely upon the professional activity in a single case, but are the product of a web of factors. In this social world the opportunity for a holistic assessment of need was limited for a number of reasons:

- The agency sought to reserve a unique and elite place for itself in the universe of child welfare agencies.
- The agency worked to give each child's situation a 'special' mental health spin by describing situations in a language reserved to those workers.
- Their gaze was extremely limited. There was no peripheral, wide-angle or telescopic view. The accounting process created a microscopic world. Children became objects to which things were done. Significance was limited to the child's inner world.

These processes produced very powerful ways of managing children.

The 'decision-making sphere' and 'congress' are simple tools which 'should remove some of the opacity that accompanies professional decision taking, by identifying factors that are influencing activity'.

Immersion in this world has produced some powerful lessons about how professionals work together, about a significant area of abuse of children's rights, and some major concerns about the fitness for purpose of child mental health services. More generally, the analysis produced a call for radical change in the organisation and provision of social welfare. The imperialism of 'designer problem solvers' (glossary) – the professionals within organizations – has been striking. Without the exercise of a moral responsibility to face up to their inadequacies and differences, professionals can be technological fascists. These actors need to be seeded in the niches of agencies to which they are accountable, offering their 'difference' into them rather than dominating them. This will foster effective partnerships between professionals, and with users.

Child Mental Health Services

This ethnography speaks to the existing services and to commissioner/purchasers (Knitzner, 1993; NHS/HAS, 1995). It is an illustration of:

- the pitfalls of government without a constitution; and
- how organizations survive in eras of uncoordinated service development.

Child mental health services have developed in an ecological niche at the 'hard end' of child welfare work.

The philosophy of all services provided for children in the UK must be consonant with the Children Act 1989. Practice must be rigorously democratic, pluralistic and interdisciplinary. Rules of confidentiality must be replaced by mandatory information sharing within a context of respect for privacy. In large part, the service studied acted as an 'alternative' Social Services

Department, but it was ungenerous and dilatory in assisting outside agencies. Suggesting, as the thematic review does (NHS/HAS, 1995), that CAMHSs should endeavour to give support to other agencies like Social Services, residential units and so on, will not be sufficient. Service level agreements will be essential to ensure that that CAMHTs do not avoid working outside their boundaries. Open systems of recording, accountability and complaint are also necessary. Interagency gatekeeping strategies must take account of 'information transfer' and 'case control' trajectories. Evaluators need to test rigorously how successfully assessment is separated from treatment, and how far the service is making the consumer fit its resources. Joint agency collaboration should aim to reduce 'overtreatment' and inappropriate case retention.

Inevitably, the data has led to strong reservations about the utility of this service. The implementation of the restructuring proposed in *Together We Stand* (NHS/HAS, 1995) is sustaining and enlarging an agency, which, if the findings of this research project are commonplace, should be disaggregated. Such secret worlds are archaic, past their sell by date, and represent a mighty and expensive sledgehammer to crack nuts. Survival in the continuing absence of a sound evidence base is unsupportable.

True for Us?

At the very least, insouciant managers should assess local performance to test the extent to which the findings are applicable to their agency (DH, 1995). More generally research into the outcomes produced by the service is vital. The users should be instrumental in creating the research agenda, designs and evaluation.

The notion of mental disorder should be rigorously reserved for the small (less than ten per cent) group of children to whom it applies (Rutter, 1973; NHS/HAS, 1995). The parameters must be agreed by all agencies engaged in child welfare services. *Together We Stand* recommends restricting services to those with mental disorder coupled with health related issues only. Yet it is also driving industrial growth with the establishment of 'primary mental health workers' as 'tier one' out-posted service providers. Their clientele are children with emotional and behavioural disorders. This may create a multitude of 'closed-complex' systems (Chapter X) dominated by psychiatric dogma. This reorganisation is a form of insurance. Expanding the service is a post-millennial survival tactic which will 'catch' excessive numbers of children without the evidence base to support it. Instead of expansion and development, the next few years should be devoted to collating a national profile of the various guises of CAMHSs and evaluating the outcomes of their performance. Undoubtedly, it will reveal extensive idiosyncrasy. Following this national audit, a service specification could bring order to the diversity produced by particular coalitions of individuals. National coordination must take full account of the needs of children and the contribution of other agencies to their welfare. Growth should only follow demonstrable utility. *Together We Stand* has missed an opportunity to take stock. Instead, the implementation, will shore up and extend a house built on sand. The current service is so powerful that demolition will need significant political conviction from the Department of Health – another form of challenging behaviour.

Children's Rights

> Children aged under eighteen make-up nearly a quarter of the population, but because of their immaturity, they have no formal voice in matters concerning their well-being.
>
> Audit Commission, 1994, p.1

Children involved with CAMHSs are forgotten. With the exception of the few children who are subject to the Mental Health Act (1983), children are effectively 'accommodated' in residential psychiatric units (Sect 20, CA, 1989). This is just as if the parent had requested the Social Services Department to provide substitute care, but the difference is that these children are not protected from malpractice by policies and guidelines derived from the Children Act 1989 (Children's Legal Centre, 1991). Without advocates, they rely on a service with minimum accountability. Fortunately, in general, the children in the study appeared to appreciate the corporate effort invested in giving them attention, care, protection, and support. Nevertheless, the regulations and guidance offered to children's homes (Sect 63, Children Act, 1989), and the statutes regulating admission to secure units (Sects 25 and 53, Children Act, 1989) should be applied. Admissions and reviews administered by a multi-agency panel, could ensure the selection of the most appropriate services. To prevent their needs being translated to match prevailing ideologies and available resources, children's civil and legal rights must inform therapeutic endeavour.

Critics of adult mental health services highlighted their disciplinary activity (Bolton et al., 1991; Parton, 1994; Sedgwick, 1992). Social policies and a post-Freudian milieu are changing the service provision, and the relations between adult service users and professional helpers. Now this must be extended to children encountering child mental health services. The CAMHT concentrated on the message rather than the messenger. It has been shown that regulatory practices in the CAMHT can be oppressive and discriminatory, and the children made invisible by an unnecessarily complicated discourse.

The most unexpected finding was that this very secret place (HAS, 1986) did not provide a safe place to listen to the secrets held by children. Consequently, children continued to *act out* rather than talk about their distress and tried to make themselves safer by picking up the clues and signals unwittingly given out by their assessors.

A rule known to the adults about confidentiality could not overcome the children's reluctance to place themselves in jeopardy. Unless contraindicated, children have a right to know how information will be shared and to know on which matters they can make choices. Agencies should respect children's rights to privacy, but no advantages to a 'rule of confidentiality' have been found. Indeed, it concealed poor practice.

Children show us that their circumstances are distressing or intolerable by using a limited repertoire of behaviours. The lives of many children are less than the variety of best that have been developed in late twentieth century Britain, still less than in the international community (Bullock, 1992). They have a right to require that practitioners do them no harm (Children Act, 1989; Taylor A A, 2000). Many agencies express their achievements and measure their purposefulness by giving a gift of some service that is uniquely theirs, and this process has been thoroughly illustrated. Much more importance should be placed on the skills and practices needed to intervene as little as possible. There are rarely right answers in the business of child welfare. Answers are socially constructed approximations. Hence the importance of having guidelines, a theory of practice (Jones, 1991), and a set of values against which to test whether the best has been done for the child. Most importantly, organisations must support workers to work safely but for as long as possible with appropriate levels of risk, and not immediately resort to solutions which carry unnecessary cost for the child.

The impediments to the integration of agencies affording social care to vulnerable children are legion, and particularly characteristic of child and adolescent mental health services. Yet a holistic approach is essential if the tendency to escalate the services given is to be resisted. In the absence of inter-organisational restructuring groups can remove the agency barriers more effectively than individuals. 'Congress' as a forum for harmonious assessment and decision taking, may be a way forward, though there remain efficiency issues to be evaluated. Perhaps that idea could be expressed as 'no intervention without a convention'.

A Postmillennial Vision for Children's Services

A 'micro' social world (Silverman, 1985) has shown how akin the business of childcare Social Services and child mental health services are, and suggested some fundamental ingredients for children's services in the twenty-first century.

Children in distress are being artificially pigeonholed into specific agencies by the artful use of language. Joint agency coordination is in vogue as a means of achieving effective and efficient services. This is ensuring longevity and suffocating the development of new and more appropriate universes.

Radical dismantling of monolithic institutions is necessary. Tinkering with the most challenging children is ineffective. It is putting the cart before the horse and a strategy to avoid community responsibilities. Most children in difficulty are acting as barometers for their impoverished environments. Parenting those universes will touch many children and their carers, and act as a nurturing and enriching wellspring. The ethnography lends support to the vision of fully integrated services, and the construction of a post-modern universe of children's services. Such a collective 'earth parent', for families and children will, in the short-term, produce some casualties. Inevitably, there is a price to pay for the implementation of radical proposals (Walker, 1993). It is the young people who are now in difficulty who may be lost in the ensuing maelstrom and entropy. However, the state is not providing well for its most challenging children, and compounds their difficulties by confirming through inadequate responses that they and their situation are overwhelming, unmanageable, even frightening. Many children currently involved with services only receive 'first aid', which makes it a good time to concentrate on global change. The application of 'triage' in this social care emergency would produce three groups of children:

- those where investment will produce a good outcome;
- those for whom nothing appears to work; and
- a large group who could be prevented from becoming clients if their environment was enriched.

A simple, child and family friendly architecture of care is needed. In this paradigm, 'professional' intervention will be driven by minimalist principles. It will be accompanied by an exciting re-engineering of faceworkers through common training programmes (Reiger and Derries, 1974), resources (Cliffe and Berridge, 1989), and a new conceptual base (Chapter X). The new services will embrace a wonderland of support, 'buddies', educators, flying angels, group workers, crash pads, 'congress' facilities, off-road car tracks and so on, all devised jointly with children.

Finally, social workers located in 'child guidance', became

dinosaurs because they cloned with a powerful profession. Effective social work practitioners apply a unique blend of knowledge skills and experience with which they work with the complexity and unpredictability of people's lives. The contemporary space for social work is increasingly construed as 'care management'. This limits their task to basic assessment and the coordination of the work of others. To resist this erosion, social work must use the power of language to describe itself and generate pride in its interdisciplinary framework of theory and practice. This process of definition will strengthen if social work is an independent, contracted component of the welfare market. An escape from the historical burden of blame associated with the work of local authorities, will foster pride in the 'difference' that the profession can offer amongst those behind a virtual welfare door.

GLOSSARY

Actor	The concept of actor (Hindess, 1986) includes the non-human. 'An actor is something that formulates decisions and acts on them' (ibid., p.115). The 'decisions and actions of social actors are not reducible to those of human individuals, but depend on social conditions and political objectives' (ibid., p.123).
'Designer Problem Solving'	Author's term for the actor performing problem-solving activity and claiming the function exclusively for the agency. The actor uses a familiar design or template for problem solution.
Discourse	'A system of possibility for knowledge and for agency' (Parton, 1994, p.13). Structures of obligations which establish different responsibilities and authorities for different actors. The regulated language, knowledge, values, and practices through which people understand, explain and decide things.
Ethnomethodology	'A detailed study of the nature and variations of mutual knowledge ... i.e. ... the methods used ... to generate the practices which are constitutive of the tissue of social life' (Giddens, 1993, p.363). A sociological analysis of a wide range of features of everyday social life (Button, 1991; Potter and Wetherall, 1987). The use of language and social interaction is closely studied (Garfinkel, 1967).

Extramural world	In the empirical universe, the actors which lie outside the intramural world, but had connections to it. For example, the Social Services Department.
Guardian ad litem	Officer reporting to the Court on the needs and welfare of the child, generally a Qualified Social Worker.
Intramural world	The constituents of the child mental health service: Child and Adolescent Psychiatrists, Psychiatric Social Workers, Educational Psychologists and a Child Psychotherapist.
'Medicine of behaviour'	The author's term for the language, knowledge, value system and activity of human service organisations. It is a reference to Foucault's 'medicine of tissues' which he used to describe allopathic medicine (Foucault, 1977).
Text	Social texts are any vehicles of language. Text and textual practices accomplish 'an event or object in the process of inscription' (Smith, 1990, p.216), and produce *a version of things* (Bateson, 1973, – emphasis added). Text is highly significant in the constitution of social realities and cultures (Atkinson, 1990). Late twentieth-century Western societies are pervasively organised by 'textually mediated forms of ruling' (Smith, 1990, p.212). Institutions of administration and of professional authority are coupled with intellectual and cultural discourses to organise and regulate society. So, as part of the tissue of everyday life, text is not a separate artifact in a greater whole, but a participant in power and politics (Parker, 1989). It is constructed and determined by all the interactions of the past and the present of its universe.

BIBLIOGRAPHY

- Adcock, M and R White, *Good Enough Parenting. A Framework for Assessment*, London, BAAF, 1985
- Agar, M and J R Hobbs, 'Interpreting Discourse: Coherence and the Analysis of Ethnographic Interviews' in *Discourse Processes 5*, 1982, pp.1–32
- Aldgate, J, 'Foster Families and Residential Care for Older Children: Some Interpersonal Dynamics' in *Children and Society 3(1)*, 1989, pp.19–36
- Aldgate, J, 'Partnership with Parents: Fantasy or Reality' in *Adoption and Fostering 15(2)*, pp.32–7
- Aldgate, J, M Colton and C Heath, 'Educational Attainment of Children in Care 1987–90. A Longitudinal study' in Department of Social Administration, University of Oxford
- Atkinson, P, *The Ethnographic Imagination: Textual Constructions of Reality*, London, Routledge, 1990
- Audit Commission, *Seen but Not Heard. Coordinating Community Child Health and Social Services for Children in Need. Executive Summary*, London, HMSO, 1994
- Bagley, C and R Ramsey, 'Sexual Abuse in Childhood. Psychosocial Outcomes and Implications for Social Work Practice' in *Social Work and Human Sexuality 4*, 1985, pp.33–47
- Baker, H and V Wills, 'School Phobia, Classification and Treatment' in *British Journal of Psychiatry 132*, 1978, pp.492–9
- Barask, R, 'Hospitalisation of Emotionally Disturbed Children. Who Gets Hospitalised and Why?' in *American Journal of Orthopsychiatry 56*, 1986, pp.317–19
- Barker, P, *Can Care Prevent Childcare or Child Psychiatry?* Herts, National Children's Home, 1973
- Barker, P, (ed.), *The Residential Psychiatric Treatment of Children*, London, Crosby Lockwood Staples, 1974

- Bateson, G, *Man and Nature. A Necessary Unity*, GB, Wildwood House, 1979
- Bentovim, A, G Gorrell-Barnes and A Cooklin, *Family Therapy. Complimentary Frameworks of Theory and Practice*, London, Academic, 1987
- Berg, I, 'The Construction of Medical Disposals. Medical Sociology and Medical Problem Solving in Clinical Practice' in *Sociology of Health and Illness 14(2)*, 1992, pp.151–80
- Berg, I, 'When Truants and School Refusers Grow Up' in *British Journal of Psychiatry 141*, 1982, pp.208–10
- Berger, P and T Luckman, *The Social Construction of Reality*, England, Penguin, 1966
- Blagg, N, *School Phobia and its Treatment*, Beckenham, Kent, Crook Helm, 1987
- Blom Cooper, L, H L Hally and E Murphy, *The Falling Shadow. One Patient's Mental Health Care 1978–1993*, London, Duckworth, 1995
- Bosk, C L, 'Forgive and Remember: Managing Medical Failure' in Dowie, J and E Elstein, (eds) *Professional Judgement. A Reader in Clinical Decision Making*, Milton Keynes, Open University, 1988, pp.522–44
- Bowlby, J, *Attachment and Loss. Volume 2 Separation: Anxiety and Anger*, (Reissue 1981), GB, Penguin, 1973
- Breunlin, D, C Breunlin, D Kearns and W Russell, 'A Review of the Literature on Family Therapy with Adolescents 1979–87' in *Journal of Adolescence 11*, 1988, pp.309–34
- Brimblecombe, F, M Hoghughi and I Tripp, 'A New Covenant for Adolescents in Crisis' in *Social Care Update 3(2)*, 1989, pp.168–80
- Brumberg, J, 'Chlorotic Girls 1870–1920. A Historical Perspective on Female Adolescence' in *Child Development 53*, 1982, pp.468–77
- Bryer, M, *Planning in Childcare. A Guide for Team Leaders and Their Teams*, London, BAAF, 1988
- Bryce, G and D Baird, 'Precipitating a Crisis: Family Therapy and Adolescent School Refusers' in *Journal of Adolescence 9*, 1986, pp.199–213
- Bullock, R (ed.), *Problem Adolescents: An International View* London, Whiting and Birch, 1986

- Bullock, R, M Little and S Millham, 'Residential Care for Children' in *A Review of the Research*, London, IB4SO, 1993
- Button, G, *Ethnomethodology in the Human Sciences*, London, Cambridge, 1991
- Cain, M, *Growing up Good*, London, Sage, 1991
- Callon, M, 'The Sociology of the Actor Network' in Callon, M and C Law (eds) *Mapping the Dynamics of Science and Technology*, Basingstoke, MacMillan, 1986
- Chess, S and A Thomas, *Origins and Evolution of Behaviour Disorders from Infancy to Early Adult Life*, NY, Brunner Mazel, 1984
- The Children's Legal Centre, *Mental Health Handbook. A Guide to the Law Affecting Children and Young People*, London, 1991
- Cicourel, A, *Social Organisation of Juvenile Justice*, USA, Wiley, 1968
- Cicourel, A, 'Cognitive and Organisational Aspects of Medical Diagnostic Reasoning', *Discourse Processes 10*, 1987, pp.347–67
- Clegg, S, *Frameworks of Power*, London, Sage, 1989
- Cliffe, D and D Berridge, *Closing Children's Homes. An End to Residential Childcare?* London, National Children's Bureau, 1991
- Cockett, M and J Tripp, *Family Breakdown in Exeter*, London, Routledge, 1994
- Coleman, J, *Working with Troubled Adolescents*, London, Academic, 1987
- Coleman, J and L Hendry, *The Nature of Adolescence*, London, Routledge, 1990, second edition
- Corby, B, 'Alternative Theory Bases in Child Abuse' in Stainton Rogers, W et al., (eds) *Child Abuse and Neglect. Facing the Challenge*, GB, Open University, 1989, pp.30–40
- Daines, L, *Child Guidance – A Study of a Consultative Service*, in 'PhD Thesis', GB, University of Bristol, 1985
- Davin, A, 'Imperialism and Motherhood' in *History Workshop Journal 5*, 1978
- Department of Health, *Protecting Children. A Guide for Social Workers Undertaking a Comprehensive Assessment*, London, HMSO, 1988

- Department of Health, *An Introduction to the Children Act. A New Framework for the Care and Upbringing of Children*, London, HMSO, 1989(a)
- Department of Health, *The Care of Children. Principles and Practice in Regulations and Guidance*, London, HMSO, 1989(b)
- Department of Health, *The Challenge of Partnership*, London, HMSO, 1995(a)
- Department of Health, *Child Protection. Messages from Research. Studies in Child Protection*, London, HMSO, 1995(b)
- Department of Health and Social Security, *Social Work Decisions in Childcare: Recent Research Findings and Their Implications*, London, HMSO, 1985
- Dingwall, R, 'Orchestrated Encounters: An Essay in the Comparative Analysis of Speech-exchange Systems' in *Sociology of Health and Illness 2(2)*, 1980
- Dingwall, R, Eeclaar, V and T Murray, *The Protection of Children. State Intervention and Family Life*, London, Blackwell, 1983
- Dowie, J and A Elstein, *Professional Judgement. A Reader in Clinical Decision Making*, GB, Cambridge University, 1988
- Early, T and J Portner, 'Families with Children with Emotional Disorders. A Review of the Literature' in *Social Work 38(6)*, 1993, pp.743–51
- Eddy, D, 'Variations in Physician Practice: The Role of Uncertainty' in Dowie, J and A Elstein, (eds) *Professional Judgement. A Reader in Clinical Decision Making*, Milton Keynes, Open University, 1988, pp.45–60
- England, H, *Social Work as Art. Making Sense for Good Practice*, London, Allen Unwin, 1986
- Fielding, I, 'Coding and Managing Data' in Gilbert, N (ed.), *Researching Social Life*, London, Sage, 1993, pp.218–39
- Fielding, N, 'Ethnography' in Gilbert, N (ed.), *Researching Social Life*, London, Sage, 1993, pp.154–71
- Figes, E, *Patriarchal Attitudes*, London, Virago, 1978
- Framrose, R, 'Outpatient Treatment of Severe School Phobia' in *Journal of Adolescence 1*, 1978, pp.353–61
- Foucault, M, *The Archaeology of Knowledge*, London, Tavistock, 1977

- Franklin, B, *The Handbook of Children's Rights. Comparative Policy and Practice*, London, Routledge, 1995
- Fraser, N, *Unruly Practices. Power, Discourse, and Gender in Contemporary Social Theory*, Cambridge, Polity, 1989
- Freehill, M, *Disturbed and Troubled Children*, London, Halstead, 1973
- Frost, P, L Moore, M Louis, C Lindberg and I Martin, *Reframing Organisational Culture*, London, Sage, 1991
- Garfinkel, H, *Studies in Ethnomethodology*, Englewood Cliffs, NJ, Prentice-Hall, 1967
- Garnham, A and I Oakhill, 'Discourse Processing and Text Representation from a "Mental Models" Perspective' in *Language and Cognitive Processes 3/4*, 1992, pp.193–204
- General Medical Council, *Guidance for Doctors on Professional Confidence*, (Revised), London, GMC, November 1991
- Gherardi, S and B Turner, *Real Men Don't Collect Soft Data*, Italy, University of Trento, 1987
- Gilbert, N, *Researching Social Life*, London, Sage, 1993
- Gilbert, N and M Mulkay, *Opening Pandora's Box. A Sociological Analysis of Scientist's Discourse*, Cambridge University, 1984
- Giddens, A, *Human Societies. A Reader*, London, Polity, 1992
- Giller, H and A Morris, *Care and Discretion. Social Workers Decisions with Delinquents*, GB, Burnett Books, 1981
- Glaser, B and A Struass, *The Discovery of Grounded Theory*, NY, Aldine, 1967
- Goffman, E, 'The Interaction Order' in *Sociological Review 48*, 1983, pp.1–17
- Grinnell, R, *Social Work Research and Evaluation*, IL, Peacock, 1993
- Gutstein, S, D Rudd, C Graham and L Rayha, 'Systematic Crisis Intervention as a Response to Adolescent Crises. An Outcome Study' in *Family Process 27*, 1988, pp.202–11
- Hak, T, 'Psychiatric Records as Transformations of Other Texts' in Watson, G and R Seller, (eds) *Text in Context. Contributions to Ethnomethodology*, UK, Sage, 1992
- Hall, C, *Social Work as Narrative. Story Telling and Persuasion in Professional Texts*, GB, Ashgate, 1997

- Hallet, C and E Birchall, *Coordination in Child Protection. A Review of the Literature*, London, HMSO, 1992
- Hammersley, M and P Atkinson, *Ethnography. Principles and Practice*, London, Tavistock, 1983
- Harding, S (ed.), *Feminism and Methodology*, Milton Keynes, Indiana University and Open University, 1987
- Health Advisory Service, *Bridges over Troubled Waters*, London, DHSS, 1986
- Herbert, M, *Conduct Disorders of Childhood and Adolescence A Social Learning Perspective*, GB, Academic, 1978, second edition
- Hersov, L, 'Persistent Non Attendance at School' in *Journal of Child Psychology and Psychiatry 11*, 1960, pp.130–7
- Hersov, L, 'History of Child Psychiatry' in *Journal of Child Psychology and Psychiatry 27*, 1986, pp.781–801
- Hindess, B, 'Actors and Social Relations' in Wardell and Turner (eds), *Sociological Theory in Transition*, Boston, Allen and Unwin, 1986, pp.113–26
- Hodgkin, R and P Newell, *Effective Government Structures for Children. Report of a Gulbenkian Foundation Inquiry*, London, Caloustie Gulbenkian, 1996
- Hoghughi, M, *Treating Problem Children: Issues Methods and Practice*, London, Sage, 1988
- Home Office, Department of Health, Department of Education and Science and Welsh Office, *Working Together Under the Children Act 1989. A Guide to Working Arrangements for Interagency Cooperation for the Protection of Children from Abuse*, London, HMSO, 1991
- Howe, D, 'Modernity, Postmodernism and Social Work' in *British Journal of Social Work 24*, 1994, pp.513–32
- Huczymski, A and D Buchanan, *Organisational Behaviour. An Introductory Text*, London, Prentice Hall, 1991
- Illich, I, *Disabling Professions*, NY, Scriber, 1978
- Janis, L J, *Critical Decisions. Leadership in Policymaking and Crisis Management*, London, Free Press, 1989
- Jones, M, *Accomplishment in Adversity. A Study of Practitioner Learning in Social Work*, in 'Unpublished PhD Thesis', Cranfield Institute of Technology, 1991

- Jordan, B, *Social Work in an Unjust Society*, GB, Harvester Wheatsheaf, 1990
- Kahan, B, *Growing Up in Groups*, London, HMSO, 1994
- Katz, J, 'Why Doctors Don't Disclose Uncertainty' in Dowie, J and A Elstein, *Professional Judgment. A Reader in Clinical Decision Making*, Milton Keynes, Open University, 1988, pp.544–65
- Kazdin, A, 'Drawing Valid Inferences from Case Studies' in *Journal of Consulting and Clinical Psychology 49(2)*, 1981, pp.183–92
- King, M and J Trowell, *Children's Welfare and the Law. The Limits of Legal Intervention*, London, Sage, 1992
- Knitzner, J, 'Children's Mental Health Policy: Challenging the Future' in *Journal of Emotional and Behavioural Disorders 1(1)*, 1993, pp.8–16
- Lare, D, K White and M Lavfer, 'Which Adolescents Must be Helped and by Whom?' in *Journal of Adolescence 3*, 1980, pp.265–72
- Lask, J and B Lask, *Child Psychiatry and Social Work*, London, Tavistock, 1981
- Layder, D, 'Grounded Theory: A Constructive Critique' in *Journal of the Theory of Social Behaviour 12(1)*, 1982, pp.103–23
- Lewis, A, *Chairing Child Protection Conferences. An Exploration of Attitudes and Roles*, Aldershot, Avebury, 1994
- Little, M and S Kelly, A *Life Without Problems? The Achievements of a Therapeutic Community*, Aldershot, Ashgate, 1995
- Lofland, J, 'Analytic Ethnography. Features, Failings, and Futures' in *Journal of Contemporary Ethnography 24(1)*, April 1995, pp.30–67
- Lumbsden-Walker, W, 'Aspects of Psychiatric Intervention' in Bullock, R (ed.), *Problem Adolescents: An International View*, London, Whiting and Birch, 1992, pp.34–46
- Malek, M, *Psychiatric Admissions. A Report on Young People Entering Residential Psychiatric Care*, The Children's Society, Cedar, 1991
- Marsh, P, 'Changing Practice in Childcare – The Children Act 1989' in *Adoption and Fostering 14(4)*, 1990, p.27
- Masson, J, 'Managing Risk Under the Children Act 1989. Diversion in Childcare' in *Child Abuse Review 1*, 1992, pp.103–122

- McRobbie, A, *Jackie. An Ideology of Adolescent Femininity*, GB, Birmingham Centre for Contemporary Cultural Studies, 1978
- Mehan, H, 'Language and Power in Organisational Process' in *Discourse Processes 10*, 1987, pp.291–301
- Menzies, I, *The Functioning of Social Systems as a Defence Against Anxiety*, London, Tavistock, 1970
- Miles, A, *Women and Mental Illness: The Social Context of Female Neurosis*, Brighton, Wheatsheaf, 1989
- Millet, K, *The Loony Bin Trip*, London, Virago, 1991
- Millham, S, R Bullock and K Hosie, *Locking Up Children. Secure Provision Within the Childcare System*, England, Saxon House, 1987
- Millham, S, R Bullock, K Hosie and M Haak, *Lost in Care. The Problems of Maintaining Links Behaviour Children in Care and Their Families*, 1986, USA, Gower
- Millman, M and Kanter R Moss, 'Introduction to Another Voice: Feminist Perspectives on Social Life and Social Science' in Harding, S (ed.), *Feminism and Methodology*, Milton Keynes, Indiana University and Open University, 1987, pp.29–37
- Mintzberg, H, *Mintzberg on Management. Inside Our Strange World of Organisations*, London, Collier MacMillan, 1989
- Morris, A, H Giller, E Szwed and H Geach, *Justice for Children*, London, MacMillan, 1980
- National Health Service and Health Advisory Service, *Child and Adolescent Mental Health Services. Together We Stand. The Commissioning, Role and Management of Child and Adolescent Mental Health Services*, London, HMSO, 1995
- Nice, V, *Mothers and Daughters. The Distortion of a Relationship*, London, MacMillan, 1992
- Nicolson, P and J Ussher, *The Psychology of Women's Health and Health Care*, London, MacMillan, 1992
- Olafson, E, D Corwin and R Summit 'Modern History of Child Sexual Abuse Awareness, Cycles of Discovery, and Suppression' in *Child Abuse and Neglect 17*, 1992, pp.7–24
- Packman, J, 'Decisions in Childcare' in Kahan, B (ed.), *Childcare Research. Policy and Practice*, London, Hodder and Stoughton, 1989

- Packman, J, J Randall and N Jaques, *Who Needs Care? Social Work Decisions About Children*, GB, Blackwell, 1986
- Paley, J, 'Social Work and The Sociology of Knowledge' in *British Journal of Social Work 17*, 1987, pp.1–17
- Parry-Jones, W, 'Bulletin of Royal College of Psychiatrists' in *Adolescent Psychiatry. A Personal View of its Development and Present Position 8*, 1984, pp.230–3
- Parton, N, 'Problematics of Government, (Post) Modernity and Social Work' in *British Journal of Social Work 24*, 1994, pp.9–32
- Parton, N, *Governing the Family. Childcare Child Protection and The State*, London, MacMillan, 1991
- Payne, M, *Social Work and Community Care*, GB, MacMillan, 1995
- Pearson, G, *The Deviant Imagination: Psychiatry, Social Work, and Social Change*, London, MacMillan, 1975
- Penfold, G and G Walker, *Women and the Psychiatric Paradox*, Milton Keynes, Open University, 1984
- Peterson, J and N Zill 'Marital Disruption, Parent-child Relationships and Behaviour Problems in Children' in *Journal of Marriage and the Family 48(2)*, 1986, pp.295–307
- Pithouse, A, *Social Work: The Social Organisation of an Invisible Trade*, Aldershot, Avebury, 1987
- Plummer, K, *Documents of Life*, London, Allen and Unwin, 1983
- Potter, J, P Stringer and M Wetherall, *Social Texts and Context. Literature and Social Psychology*, England, Routledge Kegan Paul, 1966
- Potter, J and M Wetherall, *Discourse and Social Psychology. Beyond Attitudes and Behaviour*, London, Sage, 1987
- Prince, K, *Boring Records? Communication, Speech, and Writing in Social Work*, GB, Jessica Kingsley, 1996
- Reiger, N and A Derries, 'The Child Mental Health Specialist: A New Profession' in *American Journal of Orthopsychiatry 44*, 1974, pp.150–158
- Richardson, H, *Adolescent Girls in Approved Schools*, London, Routledge, 1969

- Rimsa, M, R Berg and C Cocke 'Sexual Abuse: Somatic and Emotional Reactions' in *Child Abuse and Neglect 12*, 1988, pp.201–8
- Rizzo, J, 'Physician Uncertainty and The Art of Persuasion' in *Social Science and Medicine 37(12)*, 1993, pp.1451–9
- Robinson, B, *Decision Making in Childcare*, GB, ESCATA and The Peper Harrow Foundation, Beacon, 1987
- Roche, J, 'Children's Rights and The Welfare of the Child' in Stainton Rogers, W, D Hevey and E Ash, (eds.) *Child Abuse and Neglect: Facing the Challenge*, Milton Keynes, Open University, 1989, pp.135–142
- Rojek, C, G Peacock and S Collins, *Social Work and Received Ideas*, London, Routledge, 1988
- Rose, M, *Healing Hurt Minds: The Peper Harrow Experience*, London, Routledge, 1990
- Rutter, M, 'Why are London Children So Disturbed' in *Proceedings of Royal Society of Medicine 66*, 1973, pp.1221–5
- Rutter, M, *Helping Troubled Children*, England, Penguin, 1975
- Rutter, M and L Hersov, (eds.) *Child and Adolescent Psychiatry*, Oxford, Blackwell, 1985
- Ryan, V and K Wilson, 'Child Therapy and Evidence in Court Proceedings: Tensions and Some Solutions' in *British Journal of Social Work 25*, 1995, pp.157–72
- Sampson, O, 'Child Guidance. Its History, Provenance and Future' in *British Psychological Society Division of Educational and Child Psychology. Occasional Paper 3(3)*, 1980
- Scott, J, *A Matter of Record. Documentary Sources in Social Research*, Cambridge, Polity, 1990
- Schon, D, *The Reflective Practitioner. How Professionals Think in Action*, England, Avebury, 1991
- Sheldon, B, 'The Use of Single Case Experimental Design in the Evaluation of Social Work' in *British Journal of Social Work 13*, 1983, pp.477–500
- Shotter, J and K Gergen, *Texts of Identity*, London, Sage, 1989
- Showalter, E, *The Female Malady. Women, Madness and English Culture 1830–1980*, GB, Virago, 1987

- Silverman, D, *Interpreting Qualitative Data. Methods for Analysing Talk, Text and Interaction*, London, Sage, 1993
- Skynner, A C R, 'School Phobia. A Reappraisal' in *British Journal of Medical Psychology 47*, 1974, pp.1–16
- Smith, D, '"K is Mentally Ill". The Anatomy of a Factual Account' in *Sociology 12*, 1978, pp.23–53
- Smith, D, *Texts Facts and Femininity. Exploring the Relations of Ruling*, London, Routledge, 1990
- Stainton Rogers, W, 'Effective Cooperation in Child Protection Work' in Morgan, S and P Wrighton, (eds) *Childcare Concerns and Conflicts*, GB, Hodder and Stoughton, 1989, pp.82–95
- Stainton Rogers, W, D Hevey and E Ash, *Child Abuse and Neglect. Facing the Challenge* London, Batsford and Open University, 1989
- Stainton Rogers, W and R Stainton Rogers, 'Taking the Child Abuse Debate Apart' in Stainton Rogers, W, D Hevey and E Ash, in *Child Abuse and Neglect. Facing the Challenge*, London, Batsford and Open University, 1989, pp.50–67
- Steier, F (ed.), *Research and Reflexivity*, London, Sage, 1991
- Steinberg, D, *Basic Adolescent Psychiatry*, Oxford, Blackwell, 1987
- Steinberg, D (ed.), *The Adolescent Unit: Work and Treatment in Adolescent Psychiatry*, NY, J Wiley, 1986
- Stevenson, O, 'Multidisciplinary Work – Where Next?' in *Child Abuse Review 2(1)*, 1988, pp.5–9
- Strauss, A, *Qualitative Analysis for Social Scientists*, GB, Cambridge University, 1987
- Strauss, A and B Glaser, *Anguish: A Case Study of a Dying Trajectory*, London, Martin Robertson, 1970
- Strong, P, *Medical Knowledge. Doubt and Certainty*, GB, Open University, 1985
- Taylor, A A, *Secret Practices: An Evaluation of the Discourse and Decision Making Practices of a Child Mental Health Agency*, in 'Unpublished PhD Thesis', GB, Exeter University, 1996
- Taylor, A A, 'Working at the Edge of Chaos. Ways of Minimising Intervention', Chapter IX, in Harris, J, I Paylor and L Froggett, (eds.) *Reclaiming Social Work. The Southport Paper*, Birmingham, Venture Press, 2000, vol. I

- Taylor, L, R Lacey and D Bracken, *In Whose Best Interests? The Unjust Treatment of Children in Courts and Institutions*, GB, Russell, 1980

- Terr, L (ed.), 'Debate Forum: Resolved: Child Sexual Abuse is Overdiagnosed' in *Journal of the American Academy of Child and Adolescent Psychiatry 28*, 1989, pp.788–97

- Thompson, N, *Anti Discriminatory Practice*, Basingstoke, MacMillan, 1993

- Totman, R G, *Social Causes of Illness*, London, Souvenir, 1979

- Tyrer, P and S Tyrer, 'School Refusal Truancy and Neurotic Illness' in *Psychological Medicine 4*, 1974, pp.416–21

- Utting, W, *Children in the Public Care: A Review of Residential Childcare*, London, HMSO, 1991

- Valles, E and M Oddy, 'The Influence of a Return to School in the Long Term Adjustment of School Refusers' in *Journal of Adolescence 2*, 1984, pp.35–43

- Vernon, L and D Fruin, *In Care. A Study of Social Work Decision Making*, London, National Children's Bureau, 1986

- Walton, R and D Elliott (eds.), *Residential Care. A Reader in Current Theory and Practice*, Oxford, Pergamon, 1980

- Welby, J, 'Controlling the Risk' in *Community Care*, 27 August 1992, p.16

- Whitaker, D and I Archer, *Research by Social Workers. Capitalising on Experience*, London, CCETSW, 1989

- Whyte, B, 'Crossing Boundaries: An Exercise in Partnership Provision' in *British Journal of Social Work 27*, 1997, pp.679–704

- Will, D and R Wrate, *Integrated Family Therapy. A Problem Centred Psychodynamic Approach*, London, Tavistock, 1985

- Williams, F, *Social Policy. A Critical Introduction to Issues of Race Gender and Class*, Cambridge, Polity, 1989

- Witkin, R, *Art and Social Structure*, Cambridge, Polity, 1995

- Wolkind, S and M Gent, 'Children's Psychiatric Inpatient Units: Present Functions and Future Directions' in *Madjustment and Therapeutic Education 5(2)*, 1989, pp.54–64

- Woodhouse, D and P Pengelly, *Anxiety and the Dynamics of Collaboration*, Aberdeen University, 1991

- Woofit, R, 'Analysing Accounts' in Gilbert, N (ed.), *Researching Social Life*, London, Sage, 1993, pp.287–305
- Zeitlin, H, *The Natural History of Psychiatric Disorders in Children*, GB, Oxford University, 1986

Appendix 1

A Child's Drawing

Appendix 2
Shifts in Case Control

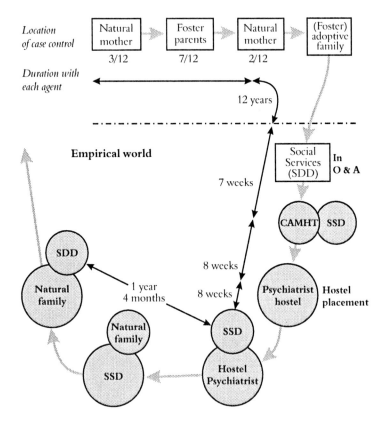

Location of case control

Natural mother ⟶ Foster parents ⟶ Natural mother ⟶ (Foster) adoptive family

3/12 7/12 2/12

Duration with each agent

12 years

Empirical world

7 weeks

Social Services (SDD) **In O & A**

CAMHT SSD

8 weeks

SDD

Natural family

1 year 4 months

8 weeks

Psychiatrist hostel Hostel placement

Natural family

SSD

Hostel Psychiatrist

SSD

INDEX